KENNIKAT PRESS

# NATIONAL UNIVERSITY PUBLICATIONS

## SERIES IN AMERICAN STUDIES

*General Editor*
JAMES P. SHENTON
*Professor of History, Columbia University*

DENNIS P. SOBIN

# THE FUTURE OF THE AMERICAN SUBURBS

SURVIVAL————————————————OR-

NATIONAL UNIVERSITY PUBLICATIONS

KENNIKAT PRESS

PORT WASHINGTON, N.Y. • LONDON

# EXTINCTION?

234514

Published by
Kennikat Press
Port Washington, N. Y. • London

*To*
*Darrin and Teague*

# CONTENTS

# ACKNOWLEDGMENTS

Many friends, colleagues, librarians, and officials have given me valuable encouragement and help during the preparation of this work. William Silverman is deserving of special thanks for stimulating initial interest and assisting in the early stages of conceptualization. Others who rendered noteworthy help are: Joseph Buderman, Patricia A. Caso, Carman George, Ann Johnson, William McGee, Peter M. Paschke, and Doreen Solce. For critically reviewing earlier drafts I am especially grateful to Mary A. Farrar and Leonard H. Fonville. Finally, for her able secretarial help, for long hours whenever necessary, I thank Francine Yon.

D.P.S.

# THE FUTURE OF THE AMERICAN SUBURBS

# INTRODUCTION

This book is about the non-city portions of metropolitan areas, the places where more and more people are living, where more and better jobs are opening up — in short, where "the action" seems increasingly to be occurring. It is about the area known as suburbia.

It is not the first book about suburbia, and it will not be the last. It does, however, have a somewhat different message to convey. The book poses the question, Can suburbs survive? This question is asked, and the answer is given, in the light of the trends of today and the expected demands of tomorrow.

Using this question as a guiding theme, the book takes a comprehensive look at suburbia: both the image and the reality of suburbia; its past and its present; its current problems and its future prospects. The book does not stop with an examination of suburbia, but includes an analysis of central cities in an attempt to identify the range of forces that will shape the suburbs of the future.

Other books on suburbia have come from the pens of many writers, among them sociologists, political scientists, architects, historians, novelists, economists, and psychologists. The concerns of each of these specialties are included to some extent in this work.

In this introductory chapter the reader will be provided with preliminary information and basic ideas to serve as both a rationale and a guide to this book. Beginning with a justification for studying suburbia and an overview of previous studies on this subject, the purpose and plan of the book are explained.

A socially conscious individual need not search far to find reasons for studying suburbia. Perhaps the most obvious reason is the fact that the bulk of development and population growth that have taken place in the metropolitan areas recently have occurred in suburbia. And on the basis of available forecasts it appears that suburbia will be the focal point of future metropolitan growth. In view of this, it is only logical that additional thought and commentary be directed toward this area.

Another reason for studying the suburbs is that they are presently in a state of transformation. As population densities and physical growth intensify in these areas, a steady and permanent impact is being made on suburbia's social and physical character. There is also little doubt that future technology in transportation, communication, and industry will transform suburbia even further.

Some city-oriented readers who are opposed to suburbia may question the value of a book on suburbia, pointing out that the greatest social crises in the United States today concern our declining cities. It is conceded that this country's most severe problems are concentrated in its cities. But it is felt that the condition of the cities cannot be truly understood without a thorough knowledge of the suburban areas which surround them. In other words, to understand the city, one must know the entire metropolitan area; for the metropolitan area exists as a total entity in the full economic and social sense of the word. Cities and suburbs do not exist independently of one another. The severe problems in the cities affect suburbia. And the causes of city problems are not confined to the cities; suburbia shares the responsibility. It is also unrealistic to think that solutions to city problems can be designed without consequences which will affect the suburbs.

Finally, there has been much confusion and a good deal of

outright misinformation concerning the suburbs. Compared to what most people know of suburbia, there is much more general understanding of the cities than there is of suburbia. This is expected since the suburbs as we know them are a relatively recent phenomenon. In comparison, the city has been with us for some time and it has been the subject of study and speculation for a period of more than two thousand years. The most widely read books that have been written about suburbia have appeared only in the last few decades and these have been novels. The relatively few serious works to emerge have not commanded much attention.

Because some attention has been focused on suburbia in various articles and books, it is important to present an overview of these works prior to discussing the purpose and content of the present book. Although such an overview will be presented here, a later chapter in this book is devoted entirely to an in-depth look at suburban studies and a discussion of selected works that have had major influence.

The largest body of literature on suburbia is literary commentary, comprised mostly of fictional writings. One of the earliest literary pieces on suburbia to appear was William Howell's *Suburban Sketches* published in 1871. In this collection of stories, the author tells of incidents he experienced and tales he heard during his early life in the original suburbs of Boston. In 1901, H.G. Wells' book, *Anticipations,* appeared. In this volume, Wells presents an optimistic picture of what he thought suburbia would develop into by the middle of the 20th century, in addition to making predictions about many other facets of society. *Babbit* by Sinclair Lewis described the realtors' interest in suburban development and speculation in the 1920's.

After World War II, as the suburban movement intensified, novels and short stories about suburbia appeared. One of the most popular books, written in 1947 by John C. Marquand, was entitled *Point of No Return*. This book is about a middle-management banker who lived a middle class life in the suburbs. It tells of the personal dissatisfactions with suburban living that marred his occupational success. Another suburban novel to appear about this time was C.B. Palmer's *Slightly Cooler in the Suburbs*. The story concerns itself with the disappointments and rewards of commuting to and from the suburbs and with the do-it-yourself syndrome.

In the 1950's and 1960's several books appeared that reported, in humorous or critical manner, the personal experiences of the authors with suburban living. Among these books was Margaret Halsey's *This Demi-Paradise: A Westchester Diary,* published in 1960. The author reveals the stubbornness, conservativeness, and conformity of her neighbors and laments that, were it not for them, suburbia would be a nicer place to live.

Several novels that appeared during this time dwelled on specific themes. Sex was fully exploited by many writers. Several paperback novels, such as *The Love Pool* by D.M. McCoy, located stories of sexual pretensions and promiscuity in a suburban community. Another volume that falls into this category for its stress on sex and sensationalism was John Conway's *Love in Suburbia.* Racial conflict in a suburban milieu was another theme used. Keith Wheeler in his 1960 novel, *Peaceable Lane,* discloses the troubles that a suburban street experienced following a decision by a black family to move in.

In addition to the numerous fictional and autobiographical accounts of suburbia and the life styles of its inhabitants, there have been many plays, films, articles and poems that have utilized related themes.

Among the more serious and unquestionably less widely read accounts of suburbia have been those produced by scholarly researchers. These authors have come from the fields of sociology, political science, economics, psychology, urban planning, and architecture. Besides those responsible for the suburban studies in each of these disciplines have utilized various methods to collect information on which to base their analyses, a brief review of these approaches is appropriate. One popular method is surveying various suburban communities, gathering as much data as is available on each. Other researchers have utilized the case-study approach, which involves selecting a single community for intensive study. Another method is to use government census statistics and other official data to perform various types of analyses such as classifying and comparing suburbs with cities.

Sociological studies of suburbia make up the single largest group of suburban studies. Although some of these studies are labeled "popular" sociological studies, in that they utilize sociological concepts and principles in superficial ways to make them appeal to the general reading audience, other works have been formal sociological treatises. Among the studies of the popular variety are A.C. Spectorsky's *The Exurbanites* which appeared in 1955 and *The Crack in the Picture Window* by John Keats, published in 1956. Both books became best sellers. *The Exurbanites* deals with the ways of life of individuals who settle in affluent suburban communities after having lived in the city. In *The Crack in the Picture Window,* Keats condemns the physical appearance and the social relations in suburbia, claiming that both are boring, dreary, and generally intolerable.

One of the earliest formal studies of suburbia by a sociologist was *The Suburban Trend* by Harlan Paul Douglas. In this 1925 study, the author discusses suburban communities and suburban life styles of the period. After presenting descriptions of what he has observed, Douglas concludes that suburbia holds many promises for the future and he predicts that it will eventually become the salvation of the city. A sociological study that appeared in the mid-1950's was *Crestwood Heights* by Seeley, Sim, and Loosley. In this study of a Canadian suburb, original data and sociological conclusions are presented concerning many aspects of the suburban phenomenon. The authors pay particular attention to the fate of suburban children and claim that a suburban environment has many undesirable consequences for youth. In 1960, Bennett Berger's *Working Class Suburb* appeared. The book was based on the author's research on a suburb inhabited by industrial workers. The author found that urban residents bring values and life styles with them to suburbia and transplant them there, rather than acquiring new values and behavioral patterns upon moving into suburbia. Another sociological investigation that reached a similar conclusion was Herbert Gans' study of Levittown, New Jersey, in 1967. In his book, *The Levittowners,* Gans displays research findings to show that people's basic life styles are not changed by the move to suburbia, and the small changes that do take place are those the people planned to make when they decided to move from the city to the suburbs.

Psychologists have also studied suburbia and have produced a body of literature on the subject. An early study was undertaken by Thorstein Veblen. In his 1934 book, *The Theory of the Leisure Class,* he attempts to explain the motivations that people have for acquiring material possessions and displaying them, and the consequences that such behavior is likely to have. Veblen dwells on such suburban phenomena as the close-cropped lawn. Later psychologically oriented studies include *Suburbia's Coddled Kids* and *The Split-Level Trap*. In *Suburbia's Coddled Kids,* the author, Peter Wyden, observes that suburban youngsters are spoiled in many ways. He finds, however, that maturity does develop because of the pressures to conform and to achieve success, other features of suburbia. *The Split-Leval Trap* appeared two years later, in 1964, written by a team of three psychologists. The authors, in a clinical manner, delineate the many psychological problems that they perceive as resulting from living in suburbia.

Another variety of studies of suburbia deals with the political aspects of the suburban phenomenon. Political scientist Charles Adrian in his 1955 book, *Governing Urban America,* voices many criticisms of the political structure of suburbia. He argues that the small, independent political districts that proliferate in suburbia cause widespread inefficiency, conservatism, and limited citizen participation. A rather harsh description of the suburban political boss is also presented by the author. Two years later, in 1958, *Suburbia: Its People and Their Politics* by Robert Wood was published. This book is generally considered to be the most extensive political study of suburbia. Wood studied the personal beliefs and social ideologies that underlie suburbia's demand for small, grass-roots government. He found that many of the beliefs and ideas that suburbanites hold are vestiges of earlier times and are no longer valid. The author also documents the waste and inefficiency that result from the suburban insistence upon small-scale units of government and the simultaneous resistance to consolidation and centralization.

The findings of another political study of suburbia, one of more limited scope, were published in an article that appeared in *Social Forces* in October, 1960. The article, "Suburban Voting Trends: 1948-1956" by Bernard Lazerwitz, considers trends in the voting behavior of suburbanites. The author points out that, traditionally, cities have been strongholds of the Democratic Party while the areas just outside of the cities have been the domain of the Republican Party. He explains that in the beginning stages of suburban development, the Republican Party held its dominant position in the suburban political environment, but that a drift to the Democratic Party eventually occurred in the more advanced stages of suburban development. On the basis of this evidence, he suggests that suburban communities will eventually evolve a two-party system.

Community planners and architects are responsible for another group of suburban studies. One early article is entitled "The Contemporary Suburban Residence" appearing in the *Architectural Record* in January, 1902. This article presents a description of suburban construction and buildings at the turn of the century. It also discusses the characteristics of suburban communities that emerged during the fifty-year period from 1850 up until the time that the article was written. It is clear from this article that the suburban home at the turn of the century was primarily a residence for the very affluent. A more modern volume about suburbia is the book by Peter Blake entitled *God's Own Junkyard* which was published in 1963. The book deals with the man-made features of urban and suburban areas, including roads, buildings, and the overall pattern of development. In the section on suburbia, the author condemns the physical appearance of suburbia for its mediocrity and its ugliness. He feels that the idea that each family should have its own home with its own plot of land is responsible for the chaos and confusion that exist in suburbia. The author presents his critique both in words and in well-chosen photographs.

While this somewhat facile classification of suburban literature shows a variety of specific perspectives and appeals, the historical interest in the phenomenon of people residing on the periphery of urban centers has been limited.

This book is an attempt to provide further insight and coherence on the subject of suburbia. Its first objective is to present an accurate and comprehensive picture of presentday suburbia. In addition to an examination of the present, the book also places the current suburbs in the context of their past and probable future. Another concern of the book is the place of suburbia in the metropolitan region and the bearing it has on the problems and trends of the region. This objective requires, among other things, a rather full exploration of the relationship between the city and the suburbs and a determination of which is responsible for what. Another goal of the book is to look within suburbia and analyze the present and emerging problems that exist there. After dealing with these, an attempt is made to develop alternative solutions that will permit suburbia to cope with these problems. In short, the book is intended to be relevant to both the city dweller and the suburban inhabitant with its multi-faceted perspectives.

The book is divided into three sections. Part one is entitled "Suburbia: The Concept and Reality." This first section discusses what suburbia is often represented to be and what it is in fact. The historical development of suburbia is traced and a comparison between the suburbs of the past and those of the present is made. Two chapters in this section, entitled "The Other Suburbias" and "The Nonresidential Suburbs", points out that the modern suburb comes in several varieties. In addition to the standard residential type, there is also the industrial suburb, the business suburb, the college suburb, the slum suburb, and the "gold coast" suburb. Another chapter reviews the most influential books that have been written about suburbia.

The second section of the book is entitled "Suburbia on Trial." An inventory and analysis of the major social and economic problems that exist in suburban communities appear in this section. Primary attention is given to the problems of the young, the elderly, and the suburban uneducated and unskilled. Also subjected to analysis are the problems of central cities. This analysis is designed to determine the extent to which the suburbs are responsible for either the existence or perpetuation of urban problems. It is generally agreed that some of the present economic difficulties of the cities are due in part to the exodus of the affluent and the movement of industry to suburbia. This section concludes by addressing the question, Are the rewards of suburbia worth the price?

The last section of the book is entitled "The Future of the Suburb." In this section, evidence of trends that seem destined to change the face and the function of suburbia is presented. The question is asked, Can Suburbs Survive? The answer is given in the light of social, economic, political and technological trends that are under way and trends that can be reasonably predicted for the future. The section concludes with a discussion of alternatives to traditional suburbs. Such concepts as "new towns," "downtown suburban centers," and "cluster development" for suburban communities are discussed.

A wide range of information sources were relied upon in the preparation of this book. Previously published materials, both historical and contemporary, were used. These included books and articles from many fields written for either scholarly or popular audiences. Government reports were also utilized. Numerous statistical data are employed, including census information and data from many special surveys. Finally, original research and first-hand observation by the author in his roles as consultant on suburban problems and suburban resident have been incorporated in the book.

To further introduce the reader to this book, a number of the main questions that guide the discussion will be delineated. Many of these questions are common ones and are frequently heard in everyday conversation. Others are more sophisticated and are usually confined to scholarly journals. But for both groups of questions, no simple answers are possible. The main questions of concern are: What is suburbia? How did it come to exist? What are the different perceptions that urban dwellers and suburbanites have of suburbia? Are there different types of suburbs? Why do people move to suburbia? Do people who move to suburbia feel disappointed? What problems exist in suburbia and are they different from city problems? Do the problems in suburbia affect all suburbanites or only certain groups living there? What is the role of suburbia in the metropolitan region? What relationships exist between the cities and the suburbs? What are the alternatives to traditional suburbs? What trends are taking place in the suburbs? Can suburbs survive?

# I

# SUBURBIA:
# THE CONCEPT AND REALITY

# 1

# SUBURBS
# PAST AND PRESENT

In the middle ages, well before the industrial town had taken form, the notion of leaving behind the complexities of society had become attractive to the European mind. For the adventurous, there was the conquest and colonization of new land and the romantic call of the unspoiled wilderness. For the more domestic, there were the family picnic or fishing trip.[1] Without waiting for Rousseau to argue that many of the ills of society were brought on by man himself, many Europeans had begun to act on this belief. Country life was thought to be best and the farther one went from the city the more it seemed one gained in health, freedom, and independence.[2] Contemporary life insurance tables reflected a belief in the superiority of the countryside in terms of physical vitality. In England the peasant and the country squire had the highest expectations of long life.

With the rise of the suburb, changes occurred in both the social content and the spatial order of the city. Since the suburb became visible almost as early as the city itself, perhaps this explains the ability of the ancient town to survive the unsanitary conditions that prevailed within the city walls. Information is available on some of the earliest suburban places. These date back to ancient times.

If we are in doubt as to the makeup and layout of the Egyptian city, both paintings and funerary models show us the suburban home with its spacious gardens. In Biblical times, we find mention of little huts that were built in the midst of the open fields, to guard the crops during harvest and to refresh city dwellers weary of the blackened bricks and the foul smells of the city.[3]

Those who owned or rented land outside the city's walls valued their place in the country, whether or not they used it to derive agricultural income. A cabin, a cottage, or a vine-shaded shelter was built for temporary retreat. Early city dwellers did not wait for rapid transportation to take advantage of a rural setting. Not only were there individuals attracted to non-city surroundings, but groups and institutions that had demands for open space and tranquility sought to avoid the central city and settled on the outskirts in little suburban enclaves. According to Lewis Mumford, not only did the Aesclepium at Cos lie outside the city, but the gymnasium and even the academy were located in the suburbs of the Hellenic city.[4] In medieval times the monastery was settled generally outside the city's walls.

In every case, the suburban pattern was typically an open one: gardens and orchards and shaded walks accompanied sprawling buildings. The early appearance of the suburb, according to Robert Wood, reveals that such things as gardening and farming, recreation and games, health and sanitation were seen as belonging to the surrounding countryside even though the functions that these activities served were directly attributable to the city's needs and deficiencies.[5] By the eighteenth century, the romantic movement had produced a new rationale for suburban living. One might be tempted to regard suburbanism as a mere derivative of this ideology, but it had older, deeper roots. The cult of nature that became popular in the eighteenth century did, however, give the suburban movement a significant boost.[6]

At the time maps and airviews of the late medieval cities

were made, evidence could be found of little huts, cottages and villas springing up outside the city's walls. As early as the thirteenth century, it was reported that the land comprising a three-mile circle around Florence was occupied by rich estates with costly mansions.[7] From the beginning, the choice of whether or not to live in the suburbs was a prerogative of the upper class. It was a phenomenon that was clearly a derivative of the relaxed, playful, goods-consuming aristocratic life that developed out of the rough, strenuous existence of the feudal stronghold.

From the thirteenth century on, the dread of plague prompted a periodic exodus from the city. In this respect, one might say that the modern suburb began as a sort of rural isolation ward. Even today, in a survey of suburbanites' reasons for moving from Chicago to the outskirts, the most common reason (61 percent) was the chance to live in a cleaner, healthier neighborhood. In comparison, 48 percent of the people surveyed gave the reason of better schools or the opportunity to own their own homes. Only 21 percent said they moved to have a yard or a garden.[8]

There is evidence that outside the walls of London in the fifteenth century people were laying out little gardens and building summer houses. These were the property of gentlemen and nobleman, places of "healthy atmosphere" and, due to their distance from the city, subjected to considerably less noise.[9] Although the assumed health advantage of suburbia was one of its major attractions, the lure of the suburbs went well beyond this. An esthetic and psychological justification for suburban living can be found in an early treatise on building by Alberti. Observed Alberti, "There is a great deal of satisfaction in a convenient retreat near a town, where a man is at liberty to do just what he pleases." Alberti commented further on the suburban residence and gave a few personal recommendations regarding the form it should take.

> The great beauties of such a retreat are being near the city, upon an open airy road, and on a pleasant spot of ground. The greatest commendation of itself is its making a cheerful appearance to those that go a little way out of the town to take the air; as if it seemed to invite every beholder...Nor should there be any want of pleasant landscapes, flowery meads, shady groves or limpid brooks

or streams and lakes for swimming, with all other delights
of the same sort. Lastly...I would have the front and
whole body of the house perfectly well lighted, and that
it be open to receive a great deal of light and sun and a
sufficient quantity of wholesome air.[10]

Beyond the search for beauty, sunshine, and open air, the
decision to leave the city indicated an attempt by many to
achieve liberation from the sometimes dreary conventions and
compulsions of society. According to Robert Wood, the original
purpose of the suburb was man's attempt to be "his own
unique self; to build his own unique house mid a unique landscape and, in short, to withdraw like a monk and live like a
prince."[11]

The demand for space changed the entire pattern of urban
development, as the need for communal security and the once-
protective fortification of the city wall ceased to be essential.
What only kings could once attain eventually became the prerogative of every commoner who could afford the land. Maurice
Stein, noted community analyst, has said that the more con-
stricted the section of the city and the more closely packed
its streets and houses, the greater was the visual relief of the
suburb's openness. Stein further noted that the early esthetic
value and psychological virtue of the suburb was very apparent
to the suburbanite with his daily shuttling to and from the city.
All the qualities of the suburb tended to be sharpened by the
contrasts of the city: openness versus enclosure, freedom versus
constriction, easy movement versus clogged traffic, and spac-
iousness versus overcrowding.[12]

Shortly after the settlement of America in the seventeenth
century, suburbs began to appear here in a pattern similar to
that which had started earlier in the mother countries. The
atmosphere of pioneer individualism led to an early distaste for
close-quartered urban life. The movement was further helped in
America by the belief that local communities should maintain
their identity and manage their own affairs and also by the
claim that the small society is the natural home of democracy.[13]

Grass-roots life existed in the United States long before the
justification for its existence was ever announced. The first
settlements on the newly found continent were by necessity small
and isolated. The characteristics usually associated with small-
town life developed spontaneously. Colonial conditions led to a

similarity of interests and a sharing of customs and goals. Under these circumstances, the independence of local political institutions developed naturally.

The first New England town relied on grants of power from the Massachusetts Bay Company and later from the colonial legislature. Early settlements in the other colonies used the medieval corporation as their model for authority. In fact, colonial towns exercised independently the essential powers of police and taxation and were from the beginning self-governing. Not only were the towns possessed of a high degree of self-identity, but by the standards of the 17th century their political institutions were democratic. The environment was largely responsible for this. The small groups of settlers were barely able to sustain themselves economically and were faced with constant danger. They congregated without hesitation to discuss an impending crisis.[14]

This socio-political arrangement contrasted sharply with the situation in the European countries, despite the fact that the forms of social organization and local government were quite similar. The democratic character of the early American communities was never approached elsewhere. In England, the parish of the 17th century was a mixture of church and secular authority. In theory, all the members of the parish had a voice in civic matters, but in practice only the most outspoken exercised any real authority. In the second unit of local organization in England, the manor, the landlord presided aristocratically. He served as both justice of the peace and principal officer of the countryside. At the county level, no pretense of local autonomy or democracy was maintained: the lord, the high sheriff, and the justice of the peace were appointed by the king from among the county gentry. According to Mumford, while American communities moved toward increasing autonomy, English localities remained undemocratic oligarchies and organs of local obligation.[15]

From the middle of the 17th century to the 19th century, the local communities of America ran their own affairs, usually by a popular political process. By and large it was the counties, the cities, the towns, and the villages that tackled the problems of land disposition, regulation of commerce, public health, law enforcement, fire protection, building control, and education. Even the revolution and the subsequent establishment of state authority by the Constitution did not at the time seriously affect this local autonomy. Although the states were technically granted legal control over public activities below the national level, most of the decisions were still made on the town and county level.[16]

The tendency toward local control in America was reinforced by contempory American social and political rhetoric and ideology, as evidenced in the works of Jefferson and Tocqueville. It was Jefferson who proclaimed the superiority of the small New England town and urged the rest of the nation to follow its example. Jefferson stated:

> Those wards called townships in New England are vital principles of their governments and have proved themselves the wisest inventions ever devised by the wit of man for the perfect exercise of self government. Each ward would be a small republic within itself and every man in the state would thus be an active member of the common government, transacting in person a great portion of his rights and duties, subordinate indeed, yet important and entirely within his competence.[17]

Forty years later Tocqueville asserted that American political authority originated in the township and that municipal independence was a natural consequence of the sovereignty of the people. For Tocqueville, the deference paid to local autonomy, within the federal system was the secret of American political success. It permitted, on the one hand, a centralized government with sufficient power to face world problems, while on the other hand it provided a broad base of power, influence, and control. More important than the institutional checks and balances, he saw the American pattern of government affecting the people and their social lives in significant ways. Tocqueville viewed the township as the center of social relations, the place where public esteem could be achieved and where the qualities of reason and good were fostered.[18]

Observers from both within and outside the system agreed that small communities apparently brought about compactness and self-sufficiency that in turn fostered interdependence, equality, and the sharing of common values. Small-town life became firmly entrenched as the American way.[19]

As time passed, the principle of small-town life became increasingly awkward and difficult to keep in practice. Even before the revolution, the larger commercial cities and towns had found it difficult to function as small communities or maintain the processes of direct intercourse among all their citizens. By the 1830's, commercial activities were taking second place to the manufacturing function of the cities and a boom was under way.[20] The new industrial life of the nation brought a steady increase in population to many municipalities.

As the cities became larger and more complex, their problems multiplied. The provision and maintenance of basic public services, law and order, and the regulation of housing and commerce were increasingly difficult to manage. There were congestion and disorder, slums and poverty and, with large-scale immigration, racial and religious quarrels leading to open conflict and civic disorder. The autonomous cities' ability to protect persons and safeguard property and to provide essential services seemed doubtful and the image of the town as a neighborhood of friendly people was being reconsidered.[21] Even politics became less personal due to an increase in the size and diversity of the electorate.

Problems plagued American government in abundance and nowhere were the problems so obvious as on the local level. From 1870 to 1900, inefficiency, scandal and corruption characterized the larger cities, while even in the towns and villages, disorder and discontent were apparent. The rural exodus and the foreign immigration combined to flood the cities and towns so that by 1890 every third American was an urban dweller, and 39 of the 200 cities had populations exceeding 75,000.[22] The signs were clear. Cities were no longer oases set in a cluster of comfortable commercial centers and flourishing farm communities. Instead they appeared to many to be concrete jungles.

Public ethics disappeared and the private ideal of financial gain engulfed city dwellers. Broad social intercourse and wide-scale neighborliness diminished as city population multiplied and as separate ghettos were established for the rich and the poor. Common standards and values were disapppearing while congestion, poverty, heterogeneity, and crime rose to such an extent that the urban world became almost unmanageable.[23]

Inventions such as the steam power plant and electric lighting had made the large nineteenth-century city possible. In the first half of the twentieth century other inventions helped to change it. The streetcar and the automobile ushered major changes into the urban scene. The daily demands for food, clothing, furniture, and workers had created traffic jams of horses, men, and carts. Now, with the new transportation devices, there was an alternative to the cramped use of limited space; there was a practical way to be a part of the city but to live apart from it. There was the suburb.[24]

The suburb was not unknown on the American scene at the turn of the century; for over one hundred years New York, Philadelphia, and Boston had been developing metropolitan characteristics: each contained a central city with a surrounding fringe of development. The population overflowed the boundaries of every major city long before the Civil War, and with the establishment of coach and ferry lines, and later with rail transportation, people became more mobile. At first the exodus was limited by the patterns of transportation. The first suburban settlements had to be within walking distance of the trolly line of the railroad station. [25]

The new transportation methods made commutation a reality. In early New York, the ferry lines and bridges made Brooklyn an attractive place to settle for those employed in New York City. Philadelphia of 1850 had half of the people who relied on the city for income living outside its boundaries. [26]

While the suburbs initially were small, distinct settlements silhouetted by expanses of undeveloped land, the open areas were gradually filled in. Two population movements were going on simultaneously: the influx of farmers into the central city and the settlement of former city residents around the outskirts. The second trend eventually became predominant. The coming of the automobile intensified the migration to suburbia. At the turn of the century there were few automobiles, but by 1915 the number had increased to 2 1/2 million; by 1930, just fifteen years later, it had zoomed to 26 1/2 million. These increases led to the construction of thousands of miles of roads. [27] People were no longer dependent on the streetcar or train. They could settle where they chose. The modern metropolitan region began to take form and the city grew outward, absorbing the outlying villages.

The suburbs came of age not only as a result of new transportation methods, but due to other factors as well. One such factor was a sharp increase in incomes in the 20th century, with more people finding it possible to afford the cost of suburban living. In the 1920's the hourly pay rate increased significantly. From 1915 to 1925 the average hourly rate increased almost 100 percent. National wealth and private production also doubled in that period. [28] A natural appetite for space, a desire for home ownership, and an American penchant for basing present expenditures on future income expectations provided the ideological foundation for suburban growth. These things were expertly exploited by land developers. Such businessmen had been a familar figure on the American scene since the 1890's, but their operations in the twenties displayed refined techniques in an effort to achieve mass production. Not content to work with individual parcels, thousands of acres were staked out and divided into lots. Real estate syndicates joined with transit companies to borrow money and plan the development of huge areas. [29] With increasing mass communication and confidence in the future of America, people listened to developers and chose to spend their accumulated and anticipated earnings to escape the city.

Between 1910-1920 in the areas immediately surrounding America's sixty-two largest cities, the population rose 33 percent. This growth exceeded, for the first time, the population increase of the cities themselves. Two years after the First World War the total suburban population surrounding cities of 50,000 or more topped 15 million. Over 15 percent of the total national population had become suburban. [30] An astounding 40-percent increase in suburban population took place between 1920 and 1930. An example of the unbelievable growth of this period was the Beverly Hills population boom. During those ten years, Beverly Hills grew 2,468 percent in its suburban Los Angeles location. [31] The decades that followed 1930 brought variations in the rate of suburban growth, but there was no change in the basic trend itself. Though suburban growth slowed down during the depression, the migration to suburbia was still unmistakable. The relatively small number of people who moved at all during this time moved from city to suburb, so that by 1940 every central city in every metropolitan area had lost population.

Along with the residents leaving the city, commerce and industry also relocated to outlying areas. By the early fifties the shopping center and the single-level factory had become as much a part of suburbia as the rows of ranch houses, cape cods, and split levels. With the steam engine no longer the central source of power for industry, manufacturing plants could locate more freely. The choice of a site was made on the basis of transportation, land availability, market, and labor patterns.

By 1955, the Census Bureau estimated that some thirty million people were living in the suburbs. In 1957, it was estimated that suburbia had grown six times faster than the cities during the preceding six years. According to the 1960 census, about 84 percent of the 28-million population increase in America during the decade 1950-1960 occurred in the nation's metropolitan areas, with the suburbs alone accounting for 18 million. The total number of suburbanites in 1960 was approximately 50 million; by 1965, it was more than 60 million.[32]

When the 1970 census figures were released, the suburban trend was seen as continuing unabated. The figures showed that the suburbs contained the largest segment of the American population of almost 205 million. The suburban total exceeded, for the first time, the central city population. In some metropolitan areas, suburbanites outnumbered city dwellers four to one. Of the 25 largest cities, 13 had actually lost population since 1960.[33]

The suburbs of the present differ from those of the past in several ways. In the past, stores and homes in suburbia clustered by necessity along streetcar lines and around the railroad stations. But universal car ownership made it possible for people to live and shop anywhere, and for builders to build anywhere. No longer were developers forced to build within or alongside existing settlements; they could now build where the land was cheapest and most immediately available. The end product was scatteration. The builders virtually ceased creating new settlements with focal points of the traditional type, with stores, offices, schools, and churches closely linked by sidewalks. Instead, the standard parts of a community were flung at random over a wide area; here a housing subdivision, a mile away a row of stores. In between were large vacant tracts passed up by builders because their owners were waiting for a high price.[34] According to John Kain, who has studied the phenomenon of scatteration, "The new developments in transportation and communication made different parcels of land increasingly interchangeable for most manufacturing, retailing, wholesaling, residential and other uses." [35]

Baltimore developer James W. Rouse calls today's suburbs "non-communities—formless places without order, beauty, or reason." They arise, he says, by an "irrational process" that shows "no visible respect for people or land. A farm is sold and begins raising houses instead of potatoes, then another farm; forests are cut; valleys are filled; streams are buried in storm sewers; and kids overflow the schools." [36]

## NOTES

1. Lewis Mumford, *The City in History*, (New York: Harcourt, Brace and World, 1961), pp. 483-84.
2. *Ibid.*, pp. 481-2.
3. *Ibid.*, pp. 489-91.
4. *Ibid.*, p. 486.
5. Robert Wood, *Suburbia: Its People and Their Politics*, (Boston: Houghton Mifflin, 1958), pp. 91-96.
6. Mumford, *op. cit.*, pp. 495-96.
7. *Ibid.*, pp. 485-87.
8. James Wilson (ed.), *The Metropolitan Enigma*, (Cambridge, Massachusetts; Harvard University Press, 1968), pp. 210-15.
9. Mumford, *op. cit.*, pp. 483-84.
10. *Ibid.*, pp. 485-87.
11. Wood, *op. cit.*, p. 108.
12. Maurice Stein, *The Eclipse of Community*, (Princeton, New Jersey: Princeton University Press, 1960), pp. 219-25.
13. Wood, *op. cit.*, pp. 21-25.
14. *Ibid.*, pp. 2-15.
15. Mumford, *op. cit.*, pp. 260-66.
16. Stein, *op. cit.*, pp. 222-28.
17. Wood, *op. cit.*, pp. 42-43.
18. Scott Donaldson, *The Suburban Myth*, (New York: Columbia University Press, 1969), pp. 154-55.
19. *Ibid.*, pp. 58-60.
20. John Bollens, *The Metropolis: Its People, Politics, and Economic Life*, (New York: Harper and Row, 1965), pp. 493-495.
21. *Ibid.*, pp. 498-501.
22. Wood, *op. cit.*, pp. 33-41.
23. Leonard Duhl, *The Urban Condition*, (New York: Basic Books, Inc., 1963), pp. 201-214.
24. Stein, *op. cit.*, pp. 94-119.
25. Donaldson, *op. cit.*, pp. 3-21.
26. Wood, *op. cit.*, p. 55.
27. *Ibid.*, p. 57.
28. *Ibid.*, p. 29.
29. William Dobriner (ed.), *The Suburban Community*, (New York: Putnam, 1958), pp. 68-74.
30. Donaldson, *op. cit.*, pp. 23-39.

31. W. C. Hallenbeck, *American Urban Communities*, (New York: Harper and Brothers Publishers, 1951), p. 202.
32. Donaldson, *op. cit.*, pp. 42-47.
33. "Census: The Suburb is Where The Action is Now," *The New York Times*, (September 6, 1970), p. 5E.
34. Edmund Faltermayer, "Can We Cope With The Coming Suburban Explosion," *Fortune*, Vol. 74, (September, 1966), pp. 147-151.
35. John F. Kain, "The Distribution and Movement of Jobs and Industry," *The Metropolitan Enigma*, (ed.) James Q. Wilson, (Cambridge, Massachusetts: Harvard University Press, 1968), pp. 1-39.
36. Paul McBroom, "New Towns: An Urban Frontier," *Science News*, Vol. 92, (July 15, 1967), pp. 64-65.

# 2

# STUDIES OF SUBURBS

Writers, both of the scholarly and the popular variety, have condemned, praised, ridiculed, admired, and mocked the suburbs. Some of these authors have chosen a particular aspect of suburbia as the object of their consternation and/or commendation; others have presented an overall treatise on the suburban community. The commentary and debate continue and will probably be around as long as the suburbs themselves. Because of the energy that a few authors have devoted to research and commentary on suburbia, some of the more significant efforts will be discussed in this chapter.

The first volume to be considered is *The Exurbanites* by Auguste Spectorsky which appeared in 1955. This book has been widely read. Spectorsky refers to exurbanites as a group which inhabits the furthest points of the suburbs and the members of which are all, to some degree, affluent. He deals with such topics as commuter difficulties, financial entanglements, family problems, leisure time, and informal group life.

Most exurbanites are involved in the communications, advertising, or entertainment fields, and share the desire to escape the "rat race" of the business world. Certain life styles are peculiar to them. Most exurbs, according to Spectorsky, were old communities which were later filled in with farms, country estates, and summer cottages. The first wave of exurbanites were successful artists, writers, and editors.

Spectorsky found that various exurbs have different traditions and features that appeal to different tastes. Bucks County, Pennsylvania, is the most rural exurb, he states. Its rural flavor is internalized by exurbanites to the degree that many become part-time farmers. Fairfield County, New Jersey, on the other hand, is high in commercial occupations and Spectorsky sees its people as compulsive socializers. In Rockland County, New York, he finds that people are particularly successful and individualistic; socializing is more selective and informal, and secluding oneself altogether is not uncommon. On the North Shore of Long Island and in Westchester, New York, Spectorsky sees a tendency to conform, following a pattern that had previously existed in these former enclaves of upper class society.

Occupational status, for the exurbanite, is extremely important, finds Spectorsky. He correlates types of occupation with certain predispositions in social patterns and personal behavior. The exurbanites who spend their days in the communications field of symbol-creation and manipulation show a desire to escape to the world of concrete "things" and rustic comforts.

Because the communications industry is extremely competitive, an uncertainty regarding how a person is viewed by superiors and peers is prevalent. The insecurity that results manifests itself in a desire to have the "right" car, home, parties, and other personal features. It is even present, claims the author, in a kind of pecking order that exists on commuter trains. The exurbanite is always living beyond his means in order to improve and then preserve his image.

Largely creative and artistic people, exurbanites sought self-expression in choosing their non-city habitat. But exurbia turned out to be a trap as the rat race they sought to escape intensified. Spectorsky also paints an equally dreary picture of the exurban housewife. She is bored, impatient, and dominated by rigid schedules stemming from cleaning the house, chauffering the children and attending women's clubs. She is also frustrated because of a lack of adequate social outlets compared to her husband's city connections.

In his discussion of leisure time, the author emphasizes the prevalence of drinking, cliquing, and trying to make a good impression. The impressions he gives can prove to be a help or a hindrance in the exurbanite's drive for occupational success. Another commonality are party games which seem to be played to embarrass the unwary and release hostilities.

According to the author, the flight to the exurbs is caused mainly by a sense of rootlessness created by the abstractions and artificialities of the city. Upon arriving in their rustic settings, the exurbanites acquire physical objects that they equate with rural life: lawn mowers, split rail fences, and home extensions. Buying and planning represent game-like diversions and provide evidence for them that their dream is materializing. But the dream always lies in the future, mainly because it was designed to be a dream and functions as a safety valve for repressed hostility.[1] The benefits derived from their dream are greatly mitigated since, in the final analysis, they are plunged into the rat race more deeply. According to Spectorsky, the exurbanite has a personal equation in which there is "one constant, his insecurity; one steadily growing value, his obligations; one steadily diminishing factor, time."[2]

Spectorsky's exurbanite begins as an unusual human being. He is inclined more than the average person toward being creative and artistic, and even more demanding as to where he will live. His dilemma lies largely in the fact that reality not only denies the fulfillment of his expectations, but contradicts them. Anxiety increases in later years due to his failure to realize the ideals of his younger days. He perseveres, however, still hoping for the attainment of his dream.

*The Exurbanites* by Spectorsky is both a criticism of American society for producing psychological problems and an attack on suburbia for offering false hope. The overriding theme of the book seems to be that there is a strong connection between occupational goals and suburban social patterns. A later study of suburbia, William Whyte's *The Organization Man*, took up the same theme.

*The Organization Man* is a study of Park Forest, a suburban housing development near Chicago. This community consists mainly of mobile junior executives on their way up. They are referred to as transients by the author since nearly all expect to move. There is in fact a 35 percent annual population turnover here. The author is primarily concerned with what happens to the quality of life in a suburb as the corporation invades the foundation of home and community.

The book examines the ways in which occupational and corporate norms, values, and goals affect the social life of suburban residents. There is close identification with the corporation. Competition and the desire for upward mobility is intense and a great deal of effort is expended on gaining the approval of superiors as well as peers. This occurs both on the job and in many facets of social life. Making friends and socializing becomes a game in which everyone is required to participate. Being alone is considered to be deviant. Physical closeness itself establishes grounds for forming friendships. And friendships themselves are superficial and instrumental; they must never become too close since this could interfere with competition.

Because there is a premium placed on togetherness, conformity to current fashions and tastes is common. Individuality can only be displayed in the form of "marginal differentiation," that is, not wavering too far in either direction. The same rule applies to expenditures and the accumulation of commodities. There is an optimal level that residents are expected to neither fall below nor exceed. The preoccupation with adapting and adjusting to the behavior and values of others makes these suburbanites other-directed and self-conscious. The pattern of getting along with others is reinforced by mothers who commence nursery school for their children as soon as possible and select schools which offer a large number of "life adjustment" courses.

This book, like *The Exurbanites,* is not a scientific investigation, but rather an impressionistic appraisal that attempts to give certain insights into some aspects of suburban life. The first complete study of suburban social life was a 1956 book entitled *Crestwood Heights* by Seeley, Sim, and Loosley.

Crestwood Heights is an upper-middle class suburb in Canada consisting mostly of successful businessmen and professionals. There is a heavy stress among residents on occupational success; there is virtually no ceiling on ambition. Everyone has a very taxing schedule so that family activities are crammed into weekends. In all activities, from eating to recreating, the office rou-

tine has penetrated with its demands for punctuality and reg-
ularity. There is little time for spontaneous activities with this
rigorous and rigid pace.

The authors point to some apparently unavoidable problems
and conflicts that occur in this community. For example, since
children are rushed into adult roles, little attention is given to
them as children. Recognition is given only for competitive
achievements, not for individual physical or emotional advances.
Up to a certain point one wishes he were older, after which he
desires to be young again. The values characteristic of different
life stages seem to be ignored; no one stage is viewed as meaningful or rewarding enough and no single identity is felt to be
completely desirable.

A primary object of study in this book is child-rearing practices in this community and the effects of the style of life here
on the children. Among the authors' findings was the existence
of a conflict between authority and permissiveness. The former
is represented by the father and the latter by the mother. They
cannot get together. The confusion is compounded by a de-
pendency on the advice of child-rearing experts who also often
do not agree. The child receives conflicting messages as a result
of this situation.

There are some things, however, that the child learns very
clearly. Because of the highly materialistic environment, the
child learns early that happiness is equated with acquisition
and that new things are preferable to old things. This constitutes
what the authors refer to as the "commodity self-image." These
values are reinforced as the child is pushed to keep up with
his peers and to acquire a "pleasing" personality. One result
of this is that the appearance of success and the reality of it
become increasingly difficult to distinguish.

Schools add to the confusion of the home and community.
The ambivalence found in the homes, for example, similarly
occurs in the teacher-student relationship. The teacher is some-
how supposed to be looked upon as both a symbol of authority and a friend. Such situations create conflict between
self-actualization and self-denial. They provide evidence, according to the authors, of how home and school conspire
with one another. The greatest concern of the authors is how
and with what consequences the child is integrated into a sub-

urban society containing almost pathological attitudes, values, and norms.

Although many books have dealt with the entire spectrum of suburban life, a few have focused upon certain aspects. Such a book is Robert Wood's *Suburbia: Its People and Their Politics,* published in 1958. The book deals with the governmental structure of suburbia and the political behavior of suburbanites.

Wood labels the governmental structure of suburbia as an anachronism of suburban life. He is referring to the hundreds of local governments that are superimposed upon one another in the suburbs. Counties, townships, villages, school districts, sanitary and water districts, and fire districts are all examples of governmental units that proliferate in suburbia. Each district may have authority over zoning, taxation, roads, police protection, and public services. The result is gross inefficiency, confusion, and waste. This political structure is completely unequipped to tackle the complexities and problems of the modern world and unable to adapt to new conditions.

In spite of this, there is stubborn resistance among both politicians and residents to any form of consolidation. The fact that this situation is permitted to continue and that it is much defended is an indication, according to Wood, that suburbanites are not as organizationally minded as has been thought. It also reflects a concern for grass-roots democracy and small-scale autonomy, conditions that were once common in early America.

The desire to return to the past is evident in many facets of suburbia. Civic associations, community centers, even the design of neighborhoods with their high visability, seem to convey a desire for local identity. This and other old values that are inappropriate in a modern setting seem to predominate in suburbia, according to Wood.

He points out that this country has a strong tradition of direct democracy through local governments. From colonial days through the formation of the country and beyond, the representation of the individual by a local government was thought to be beneficial to democracy and the welfare of its citizens. This became a legacy. Although somewhat obscured with the growth of big cities, big business, and mass society, it remained alive. This ideal was adopted so strongly by suburbanites that proposals in the 1940's and 1950's for annexation of suburbs by cities, consolidation of important government districts, and political mergers were staunchly resisted.[3]

Wood examines the nature of suburbia and finds that there are indeed similarities between the small town and the suburban community. The similarity of occupations and the common bond in civic concerns are among the items that give a semblance of a small-town culture to suburbia.[4] In addition, local newspapers and the catering of local merchants to suburban tastes seem to strengthen community identity. Also similar to the small town is the suburban family orientation and the population balance found in suburban communities. Like the small town, factors such as these promote a sense of community consciousness and identity. Local public problems and community-based institutions serve to heighten the awareness.

But Wood finds many differences as well. One important factor differentiating grass-roots democracy in suburbia is the increasing use of specialists and elected officials. The effect of this is a lessening of the individual citizen's influence and effectiveness. Control over many local issues is surrendered. Furthermore, the suburbanite hides behind a cloak of nonpartisanship, a reflection of his disdain for organized city government.[5] These things bring about a contradiction in suburbia. While residents adhere to the ideal of local control and grass-roots government, their lack of real influence makes them apathetic to local matters. Government becomes automated and things seem to take care of themselves.

In the latter part of his book, Wood examines the major problems that he sees confronting the suburbs. One problem is the need for services and finances. He finds an unequal distribution in the quantity and quality of services in suburbia. These include education, police and fire protection, hospitals, and highways. Because suburbs differ in their aggregate property evaluation, which is the primary source of local revenue, the services they receive vary. Suburbs with a high number of housing subdivisions or low-cost housing suffer, although their needs for services may be just as great as other suburban areas. Many tactics are in fact employed to insure that suburbs with a high-value composition maintain their advantageous position. These tactics include zoning and building restrictions.

The relationship between state and federal governments and suburban municipalities seems to strengthen local interests and

perpetuate the fragmentation and inequity. Assistance programs
are divised by local governments for their own benefit and they
are implemented by local government. At all levels, local, state,
and federal, there are safeguards to protect local interests.[6]

Wood concludes that suburbia cannot deal with important
issues because of fragmentation, local allegiances, and personal
bias. The governmental structure here is more social than public
service oriented.

In 1960, Bennett Berger's *Working Class Suburb* appeared.
Like *Crestwood Heights,* this book was also based on a study
of a particular suburban community. Berger departed from
tradition, however, by questioning many commonly held notions
about suburbia — notions that were based on the study of individual suburbs in the 1950's and which were generalized and
popularized to refer to all suburbs. Upon studying a working
class suburb, he found that there was no significant patterning
of life that conforms in any way to popularized notions.

The suburb studied was a new suburb that had been in existence for two years and which had resulted from a shift in
location of a Ford assembly plant. Most of the residents had
moved there with their jobs. They were blue-collar workers who
earned a middle class income. About 70 percent of these inhabitants had been raised on farms or in small villages, while
the remainder grew up in cities. Approximately 74 percent had
less than a high school diploma.

The primary research method employed by Berger for his
study consisted of a lengthy questionnaire which sought to
obtain a wide range of information from residents during interviews. The information sought included biographical data on
age, place of birth, education, number of children, religion,
employment, length of employment, father's occupation, income,
mobility, child rearing, formal and informal social relations,
politics, leisure time activities, and class consciousness. The
interviewing was done in September 1959 in the homes of the
respondents, each interview lasting approximately one hour.
Efforts were made to have all family members present. Re-
sponses from each family member were noted. Questions were
designed to compare conditions before and after the move.

Anticipation of physical and social mobility has been characterized as a common aspect of suburban life. It is said that
people here expect to move to better communities, to better

jobs, to higher levels of social prestige. However, in Berger's suburb there was little evidence of socially mobile attitudes. The people seemed to realize their chances for major advancement were slim — getting ahead to them meant perhaps a shift from the assembly line to stock checker. The job of foreman was the highest position any expected. The slight fluctuations in aspirational level usually reflected the amount of education; those with high school backgrounds thought their chances of advancement were good. But high aspirations were reserved mostly for the children. Most people felt that they had achieved a standard of living higher than they had expected, and were therefore content.[7]

In matters of political allegiance many writers have stated that there is a strong tendency to convert to the Republican Party upon moving to suburbia. Berger did not find any evidence of conversion. Instead, he found increased interest in politics among Democrats.[8] It has also been said that suburbs herald a new way of life, characterized by group similarity in such areas as politics, education, economics, and religion. In addition, extensive group participation, intense daily schedules, and widespread gossip are said to be induced by suburbia. But Berger found few of these traits. Formal participation in groups and social organizations was slight (70 percent of the sample did not belong to any clubs or organizations).[9] Those few who did belong attended meetings infrequently.

Berger also found that moving into a suburban residence does not lead to increased entertaining, although the better-educated and higher-income people did entertain more frequently. But this had been the case before the move. Even visits to friends were infrequent, and particularly so when compared with visits to relatives, which were much more common.[10] Neighboring of any kind was extremely casual and of short duration. More than half the residents reported that they rarely or infrequently went out on weekends. The better-educated people accounted for most of the going out.

Although Berger did not find any significant changes in behavior or beliefs as a result of the move to suburbia, the vast majority of people studied considered themselves "better off." He attributed this feeling to a perception of status mobility; they now owned their own home and lived in a suburban locale. They had a new feeling of pride and self-respect.[11]

The purpose of Berger's study was to test the validity of commonly accepted ideas about life in the suburbs. The characteristic changes that occur in new suburbanites, as reported by such writers as Spectorsky and Whyte, were not found in Berger's suburb. There was little evidence of status anxiety, upward striving, other-directedness, or intense participation. Berger concluded that there appear to be differences between the styles of life of the working class suburb and the white-collar type of suburb. Any similarities that exist seem mostly due to economics, home ownership, and the accouterments of suburban life. The move to suburbia itself does not necessarily change a group's way of life.

A later suburban study that built upon Berger's thesis was *The Levittowners* by Herbert Gans, published in 1967. This is a study of Levittown, New Jersey, a massive suburban subdivision located 17 miles outside of Philadelphia. Prior to 1958 Levittown was a rural community of 300 households; by 1964 it bustled with 6,200 suburban families. The author describes the residents as typically young families who are economically, educationally, ethnically, religiously, and regionally heterogeneous. They represent three different sub-cultures: working class, lower-middle class, and upper-middle class.

The author participated in the community almost from its inception with the hope of observing first-hand how a suburb develops. He wanted to see especially if there was any foundation to the common anti-suburban views that suburban life is socially, culturally, and emotionally destructive, and that these and other assumed conditions exist because of the nature of suburbia. Most data in this study were accumulated over two years by participant-observation and personal interviews. Emphasis was given to interviewing leaders, members of developing organizations, builders, and civic and church heads. Interviews were performed at various stages of the development process. A questionnaire was also sent to 3,100 households, covering such items as reasons for moving and current level of satisfaction.

One frequent indictment against suburbia is that physical proximity rather than personal qualities determines the choice and range of friendships (which are transient and shallow) and that socializing disregards individuality. Gans found, however, that propinquity may only initiate interchanges, not determine friendships; that friendships are no less intense than elsewhere, and are based on compatibility more than anything else. Evidence of forced participation or coercive socializing was not found.

Suburban critics have also expressed the view that massed-produced housing creates stagnant lives. But the author points out that everyone owns massed-produced commodities, and that only the rich can afford really custom-built housing. He claims that the critics have never considered the life that goes on inside the home, which, to Gans, seemed full and diverse, although quite family-centered.

Gans also disclaims the existence of excessive conformity and competition that is said to exist in the suburbs. Many instances of conformity are really instances of copying, a group phenomenon certainly not equivalent to conformity. Other instances of apparent conformity are actually due to social controls that are related to preserving the pride and economic value of home ownership. Competition appeared to be an occupational phenomenon found primarily among the upper-middle class rather than being an all-inclusive suburban phenomenon.

The author also claims that the dullness, routine, and conformity that most suburban critics see is actually the expression of their value-laden cosmopolitan orientation that equates a good environment with proximity to cultural and other city facilities which create variety and stimulation. Few residents of Levittown, however, thought that their town was dull, except the teenagers, who did have this complaint. Another common criticism of the suburbs is that they are harmful to mental health and discourage personal happiness. Those who hold this view claim the father's long commuting trip sets up a matriarchy and is disruptive to the family life. But Gans again found that the facts negated the criticism. Commutation actually seemed to increase family cohesion and morale. Residents interviewed by the author harbored no distaste for commuting and said there was ample free time for family activities; nearly half reported increased family activity upon moving to suburbia. [12]

There were also indications of less stress stemming from status striving and competition than the Levittowners had previously experienced. Most people found Levittown more relaxing than their former urban residences. The stress they did report was attributed mainly to organizational pressure, which were occupationally determined and limited primarily to the upper-middle class. There were no indications that suburbia itself caused people to change. Changes seemed more related to such variables as age, sex, social class, ethnic group, and the newness of the community and home ownership. The most frequent changes occurred because they were intended in the first place; people anticipated increasing their family activities, puttering around the house, and spending more time outdoors. Changes that occurred were mostly due to the impact that the newcomers had on one another, not to the new location or the physical environment.

Gans generalizes his findings into three areas: (1) New communities are shaped by their population mix (homogeneous and heterogeneous groups and their interactions) not by their physical layout; (2) Most new suburbanites are happy about their new location; (3) Sources of change do not stem directly from suburbia, but rather from home ownership and the population mix.

Gans discusses several problems that he sees in suburbia. There are three basic shortcomings to which he refers. First of all, there is an inability to handle conflict adequately. This is due to a failure among suburbanites to accept conflicting interests and motives. The result is that different groups make demands on each other but fail to compromise with each other. The second shortcoming is an inability to deal with pluralism. This stems from a lack of toleration of different styles of life. Third and last, there is a failure to establish cohesion between home, community, and government. The result of this is undue confusion and contradiction.

In the final analysis, Gans concedes that the suburbs are far from perfect, but he maintains that their problems are not unique but rather the problems of social groups and communities everywhere. Suburbanites are not dehumanized slaves, but groups of people with their own identities, styles of life, and separate hopes and aspirations. Gans felt that the residents themselves were the best judges of the quality of their lives.

While the impressionistic studies of the fifties contained elements of truth and contributed certain insights, they were characterized by value judgements, poor methodology, and sweeping generalizations. For the most part, this created a distorted picture of suburbia. Later studies exposed many of these distortions and pointed to the need for objective tools of research and the need to study suburbia without preconceptions.

Both the Levittown study and the working class suburb study contradicted earlier findings and were in basic accord with each other in undermining the premise that suburban residence, *per se*, changes behavior in any significant way. In both communities studied, many of the aspirations and expectations of those who had moved there were fulfilled, and they generally considered their move to suburbia to have been a good decision. Neither suburb showed evidence of coercive group participation, intense competition, widespread conformity, rigorous daily scheduling, or the other maladies said to exist in suburbia. Both studies were in agreement that most changes in behavioral and socialization patterns could be accounted for by home ownership and the newness of suburban life.

From this review of the major studies of suburbs, a few things are clear. All of the authors examine suburbia as an entity unto itself. They seem little concerned with the social and economic relationships that exist between the city and the suburb. Nor do they concern themselves with the nonresidential portions of suburbia and the significance of these areas. They also present a relatively static picture, steering clear of trends in suburbia and the impact these trends are likely to have on the suburban environment. But the studies are very valuable in highlighting some of the major problems of suburbia and in exposing the myths and realities of suburban life.

NOTES

1. Auguste C. Spectorsky, *The Exurbanites*, (Philadelphia: Lippincott, 1955), p. 266.
2. *Ibid.*, p. 269.
3. Robert C. Wood, *Suburbia: Its People and Their Politics*, (Boston: Houghton Mifflin, 1958), p. 86.
4. *Ibid.*, p. 105.
5. *Ibid.*, p. 186.
6. *Ibid.*, pp. 279-280.
7. Bennett M. Berger, *Working Class Suburb*, (Berkeley and Los Angeles: University of California Press, 1960), p. 24.
8. *Ibid.*, p. 38.
9. *Ibid.*, p. 59.
10. *Ibid.*, p. 68.
11. *Ibid.*, p. 82.
12. Herbert J. Gans, *The Levittowners*, (New York: Pantheon, 1967), p. 223.

# 3

# THE OTHER SUBURBS

The image that most city dwellers and, strangely, most suburbanites have of suburbia is that it is composed of a series of middle-class residential communities distinguished from each other only by their respective dates of development. Sometimes suburbia is even viewed as one homogeneous conglomeration of rows upon rows of houses that look alike.

But suburbia is not one immense area characterized only by the subdivision home or by any other single feature. It consists, rather, of separate communities, each containing its individual characteristics. Some communities are indeed middle-class enclaves containing primarily tract homes of limited variety. But there are also the other suburbias. These are the suburban communities of the poor and the rich. Each of these types of suburban communities exists in significant numbers in every metropolitan region. They are quite separate communities, differing from each other economically, socially, and in physical appearance.

The first "other suburbia" to be discussed is the suburban slum. This type of suburb is characterized by delapidated, over-crowded housing, badly maintained streets, and low quality public services and facilities. These are the suburban areas inhabited by people at the bottom of the socio-economic ladder. These are the Dogtowns, Tintowns, and Smoketowns, the patches of land "beyond the tracks" or on the "other side of the river" that are immersed in poverty.

One description of the suburban slum has been given as follows:

> ... the ghettos or slum areas in suburbia today were often marginal locations during residential development. Often they were cut off by railroad tracks, swamps, or highways. In one case, a two block long stone wall was built, reputedly to mark "the line." The boundaries of these segregated residential areas of Negroes often run along the edges of political boundaries, sometimes on both sides in a relatively narrow strip. They are permitted locations for a negatively valued population.[1]

The city slum and the suburban slum are often very much alike. The few differences are normally only that (1) there is a greater mixture of class in the suburban slum because of segregation of minority groups into these areas despite economic status, and (2) the suburban slum is often composed of housing which was originally built for the "elite suburban dweller," though many suburban slums were originally built as shanty towns for the poor.[2]

The people residing in the suburban slum share many of the characteristics of the poor everywhere. Family support comes from many sources. The father is the breadwinner in three families out of five, but his earnings are meager.[3] Ninety-two percent of the men are unskilled or semi-skilled laborers or machine operators; others are farm tenants, migratory workers, or odd-job men.[4] Fifty-five percent of the mothers "work out" part- or full-time as waitresses, dishwashers, cooks, washwomen, janitoresses, cleaning women, or unskilled domestic workers.[5] Many younger women or girls work on the production line of a local industry. They are often given preference for these jobs because they can be hired at lower wages.

Income from wages provides them with enough money to obtain the most meager necessities of life; in many cases it is inadequate even for this, and they rely upon private charity and public relief for survival. Annual family income ranges from about $500 to $1,500.[6] Income varies from year to year, depending upon work conditions and wages; this is especially true in the case of migratory workers. Gifts of partially worn-out clothing, linens, bedding, old furniture, dishes, and donated packages of food are a part of the private relief of the suburban slum dweller. Much of the time these gifts are given informally to persons who perform domestic service for the donor. Begging by the suburban poor, unlike their urban counterpart, is frowned upon strongly, and, consequently, needy families do not solicit things in an overt manner.[7] Semi-public charity is despensed through sewing circles, clubs, and other middle-class suburban organizations.

The uncertain nature of employment for the slum dweller results in long periods of idleness. Unemployment also results from illness which is common here. Lack of interest in the menial jobs available keeps still others out of work. Whatever the factors, these people are vary irregular in their employment.[8] They will leave a job casually, often without notice. Employers in the community do not like to hire them unless labor is scarce or they can be induced to work for low wages. Even then they are placed in the most menial and most dead-end positions.

The individuals who live in the suburban slum are often totally isolated from organized community activities. Organization membership has little value in the daily routine. As revealed, even getting to work on time and staying on the job are not highly regarded.[9] Employers complain about their loose work habits. They claim that these people come to work at irregular times, leave when they feel like it and stay out on the least excuse.[10] Since they do not participate in organized community affairs, the hours off the job and during periods of unemployment or lay-off are spent the way they choose, without too much interference from neighbors. Leisure time often means just loafing—whether it is around the neighborhood, at home, "along the river," or "downtown." Their social life consists of informal visits between neighbors, gossip, "going to town," drinking in the home or local bar, and varied illegal activities such as betting. The family may be so loosely organized that members usually go their own way in search of amusement and satisfaction.

Usually, their extensive leisure time is spent in the community or in nearby ones, since they have little money to spend in travel. The men and teenage youths are more mobile than the women and girls; when they leave the community, it is usually in search of work or adventure, or to avoid the police.

It has been estimated that as many as one-fourth of the families in suburban slum communities are there on a transient basis.[11] These "floating" families have a more or less fixed routine which they follow over the course of years. When the family goes away in search of economic improvement, it generally carries its belongings with it. In these periodic moves, the same conditions are usually encountered, so that a move back usually occurs after a few months or years—to again be sunk in the pockets of poverty which are immersed in Middle-Class Suburbia—until the family decides to move again.

Although no two suburban slums are alike, they share many similarities. Certain common features of the residents have been discussed. Now consideration will be given to the physical conditions found here. Exterior and interior observations of houses in a suburban slum near Riverhead, Long Island, in May, 1970, will be presented.[12]

The dilapidated, box-like homes in this slum contain crude pieces of worn furniture, usually acquired second-hand. A combination wood and coal stove, or kerosene burner, is used for both cooking and heating. An unpainted table and a few chairs held together with baling wire, together with an ancient sideboard or improvised shelves to hold assorted dishes, and drawers for pots, pans, or groceries furnish the combined kitchen and dining room. There may be some linoleum strips or roofing on the floor. The "front room" generally serves a dual purpose, living room by day and bedroom by night. Here too the floor is often covered with linoleum or roofing strips, or in a few instances, an old woven rug. Two or three squeaking chairs may share the room with a sagging sofa that leads a double life as the routine of the day alternates with that of night. A simple mirror that shows signs of age may be on the wall with a few cheap prints or pictures cut from magazines. Often a colored picture of a saint and a motion picture star will be pasted or nailed up. An improvised wardrobe area, made by driving a row of nails into the wall, generally occupies one corner.

Privacy in the home is almost non-existent; parents, children, "in-laws," and the remains of broken families may live in two or three rooms. There is little differentiation in the use of rooms — kitchen, dining room, living room, and bedroom functions may be combined of necessity into a single-use area. In Riverhead, bath and toilet facilities were found in approximately one home in seven. Wells, springs, or creeks were used for a water supply. Few of the homes were heated with furnace heat; the rest were heated with wood- or coal-burning stoves.

How does the suburban slum come into existence? It usually begins when the middle class moves out of the city and into the suburbs. Business and light industry move out to cater to their needs and to take advantage of the new markets and extra space that the suburbs offer. The poor then move out to fill the jobs in the industries and businesses. Unfair housing practices segregate residential areas into sections reserved for the specific classes. When governments decide on zoning laws, these slum areas are often perpetuated.

There is another way in which the suburban slum comes about. Many migrant workers employed by farms and estates often stay behind each year to form a permanent community as their jobs disappear due to the replacement of farms and estates by suburban development. Often, when a once rural area becomes completely suburbanized, the only sign of the past is the old migrant labor camp, which survives as a fullfledged slum in the heart of suburbia.

The federal government recently recognized the problem of the suburban slum. Five years ago it adopted several measures in an attempt to disperse the slum and integrate its inhabitants into the broader suburban community. Small progress has been made toward this goal. Local governments, school boards, and zoning boards are continuously fighting desegregation. It is now being realized that only if these local entities can be fought effectively will racial balancing and the elimination of slums in the suburbs be achieved.

Slums are not the only areas of economic segregation in suburbia. There are also areas where only members of the upper class are allowed. These people are found in communities with houses selling for $100,000 and higher. The non-rich are prevented from living in these communities, unless they happen to inhabit the "maids" quarters or the "butler's" house.

These wealthy communities are often incorporated villages. They have separate laws that help them guard against invasion by the middle and lower classes. Zoning laws help to maintain the area's exclusiveness because homes have to be set on multiple acre lots instead of the half-acre or quarter-acre required in most of middle class suburban America. Three wealthy villages on Long Island (Mill Neck, Matinecock, and Upper Brookville) have a minimum size requirement of five acres for building plots. In a few places in the country the zoning is as high as ten acres. This type of restrictive zoning has been tested in the courts and has been upheld. Wealthy American families for some time have been preoccupied with establishing homes that adequately reflect and reinforce the status image they wish to project of themselves; and home builders have helped the trend by emphasizing status appeals. William Molster, director of merchandising activities for the National Association of Home Builders, confirms this trend in home selling.[13] Researchers for the Chicago Tribune, exploring the attitudes of people in elite suburbs they studied, summed up the prevailing attitudes toward homes in this way: "You have to look successful. A house is a very tangible symbol of success.... The residents regard it as a goal and a symbol as well as something to live in."[14]

A great deal of thought on the part of housing developers has gone into finding symbols of higher status that will provoke gasps from prospective buyers; and the higher-status people themselves have obviously given a good deal of thought to symbols that will produce the same results with guests in their homes. The favored way to do this, in many areas in America, is to use symbols that indicate the owner has ties that go back into American history.[15] The use of old bricks or aged shingles is one device. Antiques, in some cases, become so important for their symbolic value that they are cherished more greatly than possessions that have functional value. One of the wealthiest suburban areas in America, the Green Bay Road of Lake Forrest, Illinois, still uses gas lights. In other cases casual but obviously costly touches, such as gold-plated bathroom fixtures or handwrought items, are discrete displays of wealth.

Much has been written about the opulent and vast residences of the rich. The observer of the personal lives of the rich often is struck first by the opulence of their residences. Ferdinand

Lundberg, in his recent book, *The Rich and the Super-Rich,* has noted:

> These lush habitations, contrary to many hurried com- mentators, have more than a titillating value for outsiders. They are more than an exercise in ostentatious display and conspicuous consumption. They are deeply symbolic of a self-conception and of actual, objective social status.[16]

The interiors of most homes in the upper-class suburb are more spectacular than the exteriors, which are mostly impressive in their dimensions.[17] Rooms are often of palace-like proportions with marble walls covered by expensive paintings and tapestries. Rare Oriental draperies and rugs, entire imported paneled rooms from European chateaux and expensive bric-a-brac and furniture are abundant. The more elaborate residences may be classified as estates. In addition to the mansions with dozens of rooms, these residences contain greenhouses, interior and exterior swim- ming pools, chapels, and statuary and sculpture strewn about. These palatial residences are utilized often for entertaining and partying. The rich do a great deal of entertaining for friends and acquaintances because they do not ordinarily congregate in public places.

The role of the neighborhood in helping fix one's status has long been important. Every city has its area where there is an especially heavy concentration of wealthy people. W. Lloyd Warner's study of "Yankee City" found that the social prestige connected with various neighborhoods was so important that people there used street names to designate social classes.[18] In some communities nearness to water is a prime determinant of class position. In others, the highest points in the community are where the wealthy can be found. Proximity to golf courses becomes the measure of eliteness in other areas.

On suburban Long Island, the wealthy suburban communities appear to have some of these locational characteristics. For example, the Island is usually divided into the North Shore, with a terrain consisting of a series of rolling hills, and the South Shore, which is very flat. Most of the wealthy com- munities, such as the estate villages of Cove Neck and Brook- ville, are on the North Shore. The South Shore is made up mostly of middle-class communities filled with development homes. The exceptions to this are the few wealthy communities,

such as Hewlett Harbor and Hewlett Bay Park, that dominate
the waterfront sections of the South Shore. The connotation of
affluence attached to the ownership of property near water on
Long Island is further evidenced by the fact that the most
exclusive community, the Village of Centre Island, is completely
surrounded by water.

A closer look at the social ecology of Long Island reveals
the pattern of the wealthy suburban community being near
to golf courses. Many of the wealthy communities have golf
courses within their boundaries. The small upper-class community
of North Hills, for example, has two full courses and a population of only 350 people on homesites ranging from one acre to
600 acres. Because the typical wealthy community on Long
Island does not have any business or industry (not even a
single gas station), but only a golf course, they are often referred to as "golf course villages."

The people residing in the wealthy communities of suburbia
differ from other suburbanites not only in their physical surroundings, but also in their life styles and social relations.
Marriage between social equals is desired and actually is achieved
in about four cases out of five.[19] Marriage with a family from
a lower stratum is strongly disapproved — even the threat of one
brings out the forces of gossip and personal pressures. On the
other hand, a potential marriage between equals is approved,
and subtle pressures are brought to bear by relatives and friends
to see it consumated, for a "successful" marriage will bring
two estates together and assure the family of its station for
another generation. Divorce is condemned since it acts to splinter
a family and results in the division of a family fortune. Children
are desired, but only one or two; too many children break
estates into too many pieces.

Accumulated wealth and large annual incomes provide these
families with the highest economic standing in suburbia. Often
they are the owners of the banks, large industries, newspapers,
and office buildings. Although the men are almost exclusively
engaged in large business, a few are independent professionals
who have either been born into this stratum or have married
into it; rarely are there cases in which they have moved into
it by personal effort.

Large tax bills accompany expensive homes and large acre-
age. Consequently, these families have a direct interest in keep-

ing assessments and tax rates low.[20] They accomplish this effectively through control of the major political party organization on the village, township and county levels. The candidates for public office are generally not members of the very wealthy group, but they are financially backed and sometimes even chosen by members. Money, legal talent, and political office are instruments used to translate interests into effective power.[21] This power is utilized to prevent rising tax rates by exerting influence against issues which involve public improvements, such as new public buildings, schools, roads, and welfare programs. This behind-the-scenes control results in the formulation of conservative policies and the election of officials who act in the capacity of agents for the interests of the rich. A large number of devices are used by the suburban rich to keep their taxes low. One technique is to have most of their property assessed as vacant land. This is done by dividing the property into two or more lots so that the residence falls into only one lot. This becomes the only lot that is assessed as improved property. The device, if used by the average suburbanite, is tantamount to the front lawn and backyard assessed as vacant lots; but the small-lot homeowner cannot do this because of the way the zoning laws are generally written.

Although the rich have the highest standard of living, their level of consumption does not exhaust their incomes; so a sizeable proportion is saved.[22] All homes are owned outright; many have been inherited. Practically every family owns at least two or three cars. Leisure, not labor, is dignified; consequently as little time as possible is devoted to making a living.[23] Wealth invested in lands, securities, and business assures the family a secure income with a minimum of effort. The wealthier families have managers who supervise their holdings. Almost all families keep at least one full-time maid who does the daily chores of cooking, cleaning, washing, and ironing and hire an additional woman part-time to do the heavy cleaning. Yard men do the gardening in the summer months and "fire the furnace" in the winter. This hired help frees both the men and the women from the confining requirements of keeping the residence and grounds in order. The free time thus gained is used in many different ways. Travel is an avidly followed leisure pursuit.[24]

Curiosity in any form by an outsider is considered to be the height of bad-breeding and a violation of the social code.

However, the rich have no hesitation about inquiring into the affairs of people who rank lower than themselves.

The rich of suburbia are a breed of suburbanites who differ as greatly from the standard image of the suburban dweller as do the suburban poor. The extravagant and exclusive communities in which they segregate themselves comprise another variety of "the other suburbias."

## NOTES

1. Leonard Blumberg and Michael Lalli, "Little Ghettos: A Study of Negroes in the Suburbs," *Phylon*, Vol. 21, (Summer, 1966), p. 125.
2. Leo F. Schnore, "Socio-Economic Status of Cities and Suburbs," *American Sociology Review*, Vol. 28, No. 1, (February 1963), p. 84.
3. Irwin Deutscher and Elizabeth Thompson, *Down Among the People: Encounters with the Poor*, (New York: Basic Books, Inc., 1968), pp. 127-54.
4. John Legett, *Class, Race and Labor*, (New York: Oxford University Press, 1968), pp. 96-118.
5. *Ibid.*, pp. 96-118.
6. Deutscher, *op. cit.*, pp. 127-54.
7. Otis Duncan and Albert Reiss Jr., *Social Characteristics of Urban and Rural Communities*, (New York: John Wiley and Sons Inc., 1956), Chp. 12, 14.
8. Legett, *op. cit.*, pp. 96-118.
9. *Ibid.*, p. 123.
10. *Ibid.*, p. 123.
11. Peter Marris, *Dilemmas of Social Reform*, (New York: Atherton Press, 1962), pp. 894-940.
12. These observations were made for the author by Miss Doreen Solce.
13. Auguste C. Spectorsky, *The Exurbanites*, (Philadelphia: Lippincott, 1955), p. 24.
14. T.B. Bottomore, *Elites and Society*, (New York: Basic Books, Inc., 1964), pp. 28-33.
15. Lloyd Warner and Kenneth Meeker, *Social Class in America*, (Chicago: Science Research Associates, 1949), pp. 34-8.
16. Ferdinand Lundberg, *The Rich and The Super-Rich*, (New York: Lyle Stuart Inc., 1968), p. 677.
17. *Ibid.*, Chp. 12.
18. W. Lloyd Warner, *et. al. The Social Life of a Modern Community*, (New Haven: Yale University Press, 1946), pp. 97-129.
19. Carson McGuire, "Social Stratification and Mobility Patterns," *American Sociological Review*, Vol. 15, (April, 1950), pp. 195-204.
20. *Ibid.*, Chp. 20.
21. *Ibid.*, Chp. 20.
22. Joseph Kahl, *The American Class Structure*, (New York: Rinehart and Co., 1957), pp. 428-502.
23. Leonard Reissman, "Class, Leisure and Social Participation," *American Sociological Review*, Vol. 19, (February, 1954), pp. 76-84.
24. *Ibid.*, pp. 76-84.

# 4

# THE NONRESIDENTIAL SUBURBS

It has been seen that the popular image of suburbia as an exclusively middle-class settlement does not conform to reality. This image is contradicted by the "other suburbias," namely the suburban communities of the poor and the rich. These two types of areas differ greatly in physical appearance and social character from the middle-class suburb.

The purpose of this chapter is to dispel another myth about contemporary suburbia; that it is exclusively an area of residences. Leo Schnore, in his book, *The Urban Scene*, makes a head-on attack against this popular misconception:

Lying within the commuting zone, the typical suburb is thought to be little more than the dwelling place of people who work in the central city. While it is correct to characterize many suburbs this way, it is an error to conceive of all suburbs in this way. A true picture of metropolitan suburbs must not ignore the fact that many of them are far from exclusively residential areas: a number of them are primarily devoted to the fabrication of manufactured goods; still other suburbs are basically given over to the provision of specialized services. [1]

There are essentially three types of nonresidential suburban communities. In addition to the industrial suburb which is concerned primarily with the production of goods, and the business suburb which is involved mainly in retail trading, there is also the college suburb. This last type of nonresidential suburb has within its boundary a major college or university, and a large proportion of the buildings and the people in this community are devoted to educational purposes. The background and nature of these three types of suburban communities, overlooked by most casual observers, forms the subject matter of this chapter.

The industrial suburbs are sometimes referred to as production "satellite subcenters." [2] The overwhelming majority of them are manufacturing centers. Schnore describes the difference between the industrial suburb and the residential suburb in the following way:

> Residential suburbs are suppliers of labor and consumers of commodities. Conversely, employing satellites are consumers of labor and suppliers of commodities. [3]

Schnore continues to explain the difference between these two types of suburbs as follows:

> In general, employing satellites tend to be concentrated in the heavily industrialized areas of the Northeastern and North Central regions. They appear relatively more frequently in the metropolitan areas with smaller central cities, but they tend themselves to be larger than residential suburbs. Satellites also tend to be older than suburbs. [4]

Schnore also considers the housing that exists in these industrial centers. He describes the housing here as being characterized by "lower average rent, higher proportions of tenant-occupied dwellings, and higher proportions of crowded dwellings." [5] Schnore found that the industrial type of suburb is increasing more rapidly than the residential suburb. He explains that:

> In these employing satellites, the process of land-use conversion from residential to industrial, commercial, and transportation uses is apparently (1) driving out pre-existent residential uses of land and (2) discouraging new construction of housing. [6]

Although cities continue to hold a great deal of industry, the suburbs have become the favorite points of location for new manufacturing plants. Apart from the practical matter of site availability, a number of forces operate to bring industry to the suburbs — forces deriving from the changing character of industry, product and labor markets, and industrial technology.

The location of industry in suburban areas has resulted from several factors. These include the electrification of power, the increased mobility of labor due to the automobile, and the separation of production from central office functions which can be carried on independently in the central city. Other factors that have served to attract industry to the suburbs are the needs of industry for space and a modern plant layout. Industries which have operated in a multi-story building find that their needs for modern equipment, for mass production, and for more efficient flow of materials, require a single-level operation. It is also much more expensive, in terms of construction costs, to build a multi-story building than a single-level plant. Sites with sufficient space to build a large one-level facility are often available only in suburban areas.

Considerations relating to the supply of labor have also served to induce the migration of industry to outlying areas. This involves the generally greater availability of labor in suburbia, the lower wages needed to attract workers, and the absence of extensive union organization which is characteristic of the city. Employers in the suburbs also boast about the higher quality of labor here. Studies have shown that many employers prefer to hire individuals who reside near the place of work, believing that such employees are more content and are better workers.[7] It is certainly true that as the commuting radius lengthens with the growth of suburbia, the time, energy, and cost of traveling back and forth to a job in the city increases. This causes dissatisfaction and worker demands for wages higher than those in their immediate area of residence, often more than is justified on the basis of productivity.[8] Once a labor supply has developed in a suburb, particularly a skilled labor pool, a strong magnet exists to attract industry there.

John Kain reports that "rapid increases in automobile ownership have released many firms from their need to be located convenient to mass transit facilities in order to attract a labor force."[9] He presents studies that show that firms locating in suburban areas have an easier time attracting a labor force due to better parking and more pleasant environmental conditions than existed at their city location.

Industry has a self-generating quality which is most evident in the suburbs. The presence of a prime producer, such as a steel processing plant, encourages the location of other plants, such as steel fabricators. This has occurred in the suburbs of Pittsburgh and Cleveland. In the Detroit area, a clustering of automobile manufacturing plants has produced within the area a secondary cluster of suppliers of parts and accessories. The development of the instruments and electronics industries in the vicinity of major aircraft producers in the New York-Long Island suburban area is another instance of the self-generating quality of industry. This has a marked influence on the perpetuation and growth of the industrial suburbs.

Suburbia has been looked upon as an attractive market by manufacturers in the residentiary industries. These include bakeries and canneries, builders, printers, and manufacturers of building materials, home furnishings, and appliances. All of these industries have sales that are chiefly local in character. As population concentrates increasingly in metropolitan areas, these industries are drawn to the suburbs to develop the mass market "at their doorstep."

Although a large number of industries in the suburbs are concerned with the local market, the bulk of industries here deal mainly with national and international markets. These industries are found in the suburbs due to a decentralization of manufacturing that has occurred in the United States and a movement to establish branch plants, processing plants, packaging plants, and plants for the final assembly of parts in the major urban areas of the nation. Because the sites needed are most readily available in the suburbs, this national trend in the decentralization of manufacturing has helped to spur suburban industrial growth.

Strict zoning requirements and the insistent opposition of suburbanites to the location of industry in their neighborhoods have compelled industrial planners and government officials to restrict industrial development to certain areas. These areas eventually become the industrial suburban communities. Despite occasional local opposition, government officials in the suburbs have for the most part favored the emergence and growth of these industrial areas both to provide local jobs and to broaden the tax base. There is little question that industry more than pays the costs of public services it uses; one study found that industry paid in taxes two and three-fourths as much as the cost of services furnished it by the local government.[10]

One device for satisfying the needs of industry seeking to locate in suburbia, while preserving the character of the surrounding communities, is to locate industry in industrial parks. These are large blocks of land with sites for a number of industrial plants, close to arterial highways and utilities, and separated by a landscaped border, or "buffer zone", from neighboring residential areas. Industrial parks are technically defined as:

> Tracts of land, the control and administration of which are vested in a single body, suitable for industrial use because of location, topography, proper zoning, availability of utilities and accessibility to transportation... all requirements are to be compatible with the community and surrounding land use.[11]

The inherent idea in the formation of these parks is the establishment of industrial communities. The success of this has yet to be determined since many of these industrial parks, as yet, have remained simply industrial areas, not communities, within suburbia. It is clear, however, that some industrial parks have generated others in the immediate area and now resemble the beginnings of an industrial community.

Schnore observed that "employing suburbs are becoming more exclusively devoted to industry and other employment producing activities."[12] There are many instances concerning the newer industrial parks on Long Island, such as the Vanderbilt Industrial Park in Hauppauge, where a trend to exclude all types of housing from the area is apparent. Being located in an exclusively industrial community assures companies that they will not be troubled by surrounding residents over issues of noise and air pollution or any of the other numerous conflicts that might exist between industrial and residential development.

As industrial communities and industrial parks have sprung up in suburbia, employment opportunities have opened up for many suburbanites. This has changed somewhat the character of many suburban areas from a series of "bedroom communities" for managerial and professional persons commuting to the city to communities exhibiting a more equal distribution of skills among its population and more of a balance of those employed locally and those with jobs in the city.

We have considered the industrial suburb: its characteristics, its causes, its consequences. Now let us turn to another variety of the nonresidential suburb, the business suburb. The business suburb is a suburban community characterized by a high density of retail businesses and office buildings. It is very much like the industrial type suburb in its nonresidential character. Even the shopping center shares many similarities with the industrial park.

The main characteristics of the business suburb are that it is made up of offices, distributors, small shops, and sales and regional offices of businesses. The larger business areas have shopping malls, executive clubs, restaurants, barber shops, and beauty parlors.[13]

With the widespread use of cars in the suburbs, stores have tended to bunch in certain areas instead of stringing out in a "ribbon" type of development along highways. In some cases advance zoning set aside certain areas for commercial use, in other cases the development of shopping centers brought together a department store and a variety of other stores whose products and services complement each other, with adequate off-street parking for customers. Additionally, the insistence upon "one-stop" stores have favored the growth of large self-service supermarkets selling everything from food and drugs to kitchenware. The supermarket, shopping center, and discount houses have created a revolution in retailing techniques which have put many small retailers out of business or have forced them to adopt new merchandising methods.[14]

Carle Place, on Long Island, is an example of a business suburb. This community contains a central business district of small stores, several shopping centers including the massive Roosevelt Field, and extensive strip commercial development on most of the major roads in the community. There are five major, multi-level department stores located in Carle Place. Housing exists on the wedges of land located between the business developments.

An example of an emerging business suburb is Lake Grove, also located on Long Island. Lake Grove is a three-year-old incorporated village in Suffolk County that came into being because residents saw the growth of businesses there and wanted to capitalize on the tax advantages this could bring. A major shopping center, the Smith Haven Shopping Mall, has been built here and many commercial developers have plans for additional business facilities adjacent to the mall and in other parts of the Village. Bohack, a supermarket chain, had an application pending before the Village Zoning Board at the time of this writing for a seven-story office building.

The older type of business suburb is the "downtown" or business district serving a number of towns. An example of this is the Village of Hempstead, Long Island. Hempstead is the oldest village on Long Island, incorporated in 1853. From the beginning it was a trading center for surrounding areas. As suburban development occurred, it became a regional business and office center.

In a recent article, many advantages were cited for businesses in the suburbs, including "escape from the problems of city locations — high rent, lack of parking places, and shortages of desk space and clerical help." [15] Rental of an office in the suburbs also allows a large company to have several small offices scattered in many cities without having to finance building operations.

The growth of business in the suburbs is due partly to the spread in the demand for goods and services within metropolitan areas. Cities have always enjoyed a high level of goods and services, but the transfer of population to the suburb, particularly of the upper-middle income groups, has meant a sharp outward shift in the demand for goods and services. Furthermore, as industry has begun to locate in suburban areas and skilled workers have moved there, an additional force has existed for the outward pull of goods and services.

This does not mean that all city retail businesses have sought the growing suburban market. To some extent the expanding suburban market has been tapped by original local merchants and by additional stores, shops, and firms established in the suburbs in the post-war small business boom.[16] But national food stores, drug, jewelery, and other chains have hastened to build outlets in the suburbs, alongside branches of department stores, specialty shops, brokerage houses, insurance companies, banks, and savings and loan associations. In contrast financial and business-oriented services have remained concentrated to a considerable extent in the central city and, while retailing has sought the suburb, wholesaling has tended to stay in the city.[17]

The unique features of the suburbs have generated a special breed of businesses. High incomes have brought more doctors, dentists, and other professionals per capita than exist in the cities. The extensive use of private cars has led to the establishment of numerous car dealerships, garages, and service stations. The large amount of home construction and renovation in the suburbs has called forth a host of building material, home furnishing, and appliance outlets, as well as other home services.

It is apparent that the business suburb and the industrial suburb share several similarities. There is a third type of non-residential suburb, however, that is in a category by itself. This is the college suburb. It consists of a suburban community in which a major college or university is located.

A large proportion of the buildings and the people in the college suburb revolve around the activities of the college. Many of the buildings, including many former homes, are owned or rented by the college and are used for educational purposes. Several of the other buildings serve as homes for faculty, staff, and students, while others are business establishments that cater to the college market. These business establishments include bars ("The Campus Inn"), book stores ("The College Book Nook"), and inexpensive restaurants (one short-order restaurant in a college suburb features "the hamburger with a college education").

The college seems to occupy many roles in the community. These roles were discussed in the proceedings of a recent National Student Association Conference. Four roles were identified:

1. Investor — Public and private institutions are major stock-holders, and often land-holders. Also the trustees frequently sit on boards of directors of major corporations.
2. Employer — In addition to faculty employment, the university may engage administration staff, maintenance workers, hospital staff, building construction workers, etc.
3. Partner in, or initiator of, urban renewal — The alteration of physical surroundings, especially in creating an isolated university, is frequent in large urban centers.
4. Procurer of supplies — The university buys, in great quantities, those supplies necessary for its operation.[18]

There are various additional ways in which the college relates
to the community in which it is located. The college extension
services, for example, are designed partly to aid the local community. Where the enrichment and stabilization of the community have been priority objectives, this work has been highly successful. [19] Some colleges have actually begun programs for the
training of community leaders. This has reportedly proven very
effective. [20] Professional and lay leaders are viewed by colleges
as prospective coordinators of campus-community-centered activities. Since many communities have such leaders in short supply,
local colleges are beginning to train them. Ideally, members of
the community are coached in the know-how of group leadership and interpersonal communication. They are not treated as
a special group, but rather dealt with as responsible community
residents. Difficulties arise in some leadership programs when
training is done without regard to values and opportunities
that exist in the local community. At present, many colleges,
aside from their public relations, have not yet initiated such
leadership development programs.

Another service of the college to the community is the organization of study groups or community councils. These groups
are concerned with the development of social, economic, and
artistic resources in the community. The imagination and ability
to explore and develop local resources can usually be found in
the community, but some direction is usually needed. The
know-how, the expertise, the initial leadership and prestige, and
the broad contacts which the college can supply serve to give
this direction.

"Action projects" in the college suburb often result from the
research and discussions of a study group. A new swimming
pool, school, library, hospital, museum, health program, land-
use study, and community center are some of the things which
have been accomplished with such a college-community relationship. [21]

One service of the local college which is provided in many
communities is an adult education program. Any community
large enough to support an undergraduate college can support
useful and meaningful programs of adult education. Some adult
students prefer special programs or single courses to regular
undergraduate curricula. Some want understanding of particular political or social problems or wish to increase their in-

terpersonal skills. Others seek to remedy gaps in their education. Many seek training in skills immediately applicable in their jobs. The majority of adult students indeed have particular vocational, personal, and social objectives in mind when entering an adult education program and these individual objectives often reflect the concerns and values of the community.

The college in a community with a large foreign population plays an integral part in the community by offering courses in English, citizenship preparation, American culture and institutions, and even courses in the characteristics and problems of the local community. Courses in the structure of local, state, and federal governments and in the organization and problems of the school systems and other public areas make valuable contributions to civic life to both the foreign-born and natives alike.

A local college possesses the opportunity to become the focal point for the intellectual and cultural life of its community. Usually this is done by means of its regular educational programs, adult as well as undergraduate. But there are other ways in which the college may contribute to the intellectual and cultural life of the community. The art exhibit, the concert series, the college library, and the lecture series are a few of the many examples.

Conflicts between the college and local suburbanites sometimes exist. This often occurs when the college is undergoing rapid growth and expansion. Residents are often fearful that the expanding college will change the character of the community. They are usually right, for as the college grows, the community changes from a residential suburb to a college suburb, bringing more people, more intensive development, more traffic, and the institutional type of buildings. This conflict between the college and local residents is presently occurring in Oakdale, Long Island, where a new private school, Dowling College, has recently unveiled the first of a series of plans for expansion.

In summarizing the role and significance of the college in the suburban community, the following excerpt from a National Student Association publication is useful:

> The university, partially as a product of the community, partially as a participant in the community, and partially as a producer of the community, must place its power

behind the needs of the community. In addition to avoiding policies which create or perpetuate poverty or discrimination, the university should also enter into positive relations with the community.[22]

Examined in this chapter were the three types of nonresidential suburbs; the industrial suburb, the business suburb, and the college suburb. Each of these suburban communities was seen to have characteristics that clearly distinguish it from the middle-class housing tracts that many people falsely believe cover all of suburbia.

## NOTES

1. Leo F. Schnore, *The Urban Scene*, (New York: The Free Press, 1965), p. 138.
2. *Ibid.*, p. 139.
3. *Ibid.*, p. 140.
4. *Ibid.*, pp. 141-142.
5. *Ibid.*, p. 142.
6. *Ibid.*, p. 144.
7. Charles Stonier, "Industry Looks at Long Island," *Hofstra College Bureau of Business Research* (New York: Hofstra College, 1956), p. 21.
8. E.J. Burtt, Jr., "Workers Adapt to Plant Relocation in Suburbia," *Monthly Labor Review*, Vol. 91, (April, 1968), pp. 1-5.
9. John F. Kain, "The Distribution and Movement of Jobs and Industry," *The Metropolitan Enigma*, ed. James Q. Wilson, (Cambridge, Massachusetts: Harvard University Press, 1968), pp. 1-39.
10. Charles Stonier and Associates, "Does Industry Pay Its Own Way?," *Hofstra College Bureau of Business Research*, (New York: Hofstra College, 1956), pp. 1-26.
11. "How to Woo and Win Industry: A Symposium," *Nation's Business*, Vol. 56, (November, 1968), pp. 82-6.
12. Schnore, *op. cit.*, p. 144.
13. "Wooing White Collars to Suburbia: Office Parks," *Business Week*, (July 8, 1967), p. 97.
14. Amos H. Hawley, *The Changing Shape of Metropolitan America*, (Glencoe, Ill.: Free Press, 1955), pp. 168-172.
15. "Wooing White Collars to Suburbia," *op. cit.*, p. 97.
16. Benjamin Chinitz, *City and Suburb: The Economics of Metropolitan Growth*, (Englewood Cliffs, New Jersey: Prentice-Hall, 1965), Chps. 2, 3.
17. Edgar Hoover and Raymond Vernon, *Anatomy of a Metropolis*, (Garden City, New York: Doubleday and Co., 1959), Appendix A.
18. Diane Carleback, ed. *Codification of Policy of the United States National Student Association*, (Washington, D.C.: 1967-68), p. 69.
19. Algo Henderson, *Policies and Practices in Higher Education*, (New York: Harper and Brothers, 1960), pp. 29-49.
20. Nevitt Sandford, *The American College*, (New York: John Wiley and Sons, Inc., 1962), pp. 894-940.
21. Henderson, *op. cit.*, pp. 153-62.
22. Carleback, *op. cit.*, p. 70.

# II

# SUBURBIA ON TRIAL

# 5

# THE SUBURBAN MYSTIQUE

The migration of city dwellers to suburbia since World War II has been more than a gradual trend; it has been a stampede. Several factors underly this phenomenon.

Demographers who study population movements tell us that all migrations are due to a multiplicity of factors. They have developed a theory known as the "pull-push" theory to explain migrations. This theory states that there are two basic types of factors responsible for every migration. The first type are the "pull" factors. These consist of attractions that those migrating see in the area in which they seek to locate. The second category consists of the "push" factors. These are negative features of the places that those migrating are leaving.

The early settlers and the later immigrants who came to America made the decision to leave their native lands because of political pressures and limited economic opportunities there. They decided to come to America because this country had the attraction of open land and untapped natural resources.

The mass movement to suburbia was largely the result of "pull" factors. It is true that a certain amount of "push" was involved in that many of those who came were fed up with the problems and pressures of city life. But for the majority the move was made because of many attractions that were seen in suburbia. After the move was made, some of these attractions proved to be real, while others proved to be false.

The sum total of all of the attractions that suburbia has held is labeled the "suburban mystique." This chapter considers these attractions and attempts to determine which of these have been real and which have been only imagined. This will be done by contrasting the expectations of new suburbanites and their actual experiences with suburbia. A disparity between the "real" and the "ideal" suburbia will be shown to exist.

The total number of suburbanites in 1960 was approximately fifty million, by 1965 it was more than sixty million and it is still rising. It has been predicted that by the 1980's one hundred million Americans will live in the suburbs. [1] What is there about the "suburban mystique" that so many millions are now living in suburbia and more millions will move there? The images of suburbia that were created during the 1950's were highly uncomplimentary. Some powerful and popular writers, such as W. Whyte, F. Allen, H. Henderson, J. Keats, Seeley and his associates, and others, attacked suburbia for the physical, social, and psychological pathologies they observed in it. Yet suburbia grew and grew, and still continues to grow.

Although William Whyte was one of those writers who attacked suburbia in the 1950's, he offered an explanation for its phenomenal growth based on his study of the Park Forest suburb.

> In most cases the dominant factors for the move to suburbia were the space for the money, the amenities not anywhere else available, and most important, the fact that it was so well set up for children. Park Foresters went there for quite rational and eminently sensible reasons. Once there, however, they created something over and above the original bargain ... a social atmosphere of striking vigor. The developers were quick to recognize it and first they were just advertising Park Forest as housing but then began to advertise happiness. [2]

John Keats, in an article entitled "Compulsive Suburbia," stated his opinion that the decision to move to suburbia is usually given little thought and almost no logical analysis by most of those who make this decision. He narrows the reasons for people deciding to buy a home in suburbia to two:

> They bought their house because a) they were told a family should own one, and b) they imagined it would be cheaper to buy a house in the suburbs than to rent in the city.[3]

Frederick L. Allen, writing in *Harper's Magazine* in 1954, traced the movement to the suburbs largely to the conditions in the cities. Allen's position is that the city has repelled a considerable number of the people it once drew. The negative aspects of the cities therefore become the positive hopes for the suburbs.

> The city repelled them with its noise, soot, fumes, barren pavements, traffic tie-ups, nervous pressures, and inhuman dimensions, and especially with the apparent unsuitability of life it imposed upon small children. The move to the suburbs was to enjoy the power and glory of the city and yet at the same time, by daily travel, to enjoy quiet in the ... country.[4]

How is it that these and other reasons for moving to suburbia have remained alive in the face of severe criticisms of suburbia? One student of suburbia commented on the negative publicity the suburbs have received and the fact that this has not deterred people from locating here. "The suburban environment seems likely to survive and expand; the wish to have one's cake and eat it too is still strong."[5]

While the image of suburbia has suffered from the harsh critics, the home-buying suburbanites are busily and unconsciously combating the critics. Being unswayed by the uncomplimentary picture that some outsiders have painted, other outsiders, the buying public, are adding to the accelerating rate of suburban growth. In recent years, suburbs have grown about five times faster than the central cities they surround.

Urbanologist Raymond Vernon wondered why the general American public paid little attention to the downgrading reports that suburbia had been receiving. The answer he came up with was that, to most Americans, suburbia represents progress and improvement, while they view the cities as being at a standstill. "They see their lot as being better than that of their parents and confidently expect their children to do a little better," says Vernon. Thus, while critics who are sometimes very well-informed scholars are pinpointing the flaws and problems of suburbia, the general public appears more concerned with the personal benefits they see in suburbia relative to their particular situation.

Vernon suggests that the apathy that exists among city dwellers towards the problems of the city is largely a result of the availability of an easy escape route to suburbia.

> We may have an answer to the riddle of the curious passivity of America to its urban problems. To most Americans, the personal experience of urban living seems not one of personal retrogression but of continuous improvement. By moving out of the slag heaps of the worked-out city, they have improved their surroundings sufficient for a generation.... Let the central city weep; let the sociologist fume; except for such intractable problems as death, war, and taxes, things are getting slightly better all the time.[6]

Jonathan Black in *The New Leader* similarly explained the popularity of suburbia in terms of a desire to abandon the problems of the city.

> If the skyscraper is the symbol of megalopolis, it may also be its undoing.... Downtown towers proliferate in staggering numbers, clotting traffic, choking off light and air, luring an unmanageable mass of people and vehicles into less and less space. Blighted ghettos cling to the periphery of downtown, cancerously multiplying and invading better neighborhoods. The semifortunate take refuge in "slurbs" while the cherished middle-classes commute to greener pastures, their precious tax dollars stuffed in their Brooks Brothers pockets.[7]

Some of the features of suburbia receiving criticism are often viewed by the general public as attractions of suburbia. For example, it has been found that the similarities shared by suburban populations (the social, economic, and occupational features many suburbanites have in common) are looked upon with disdain by critics but are attractive to many considering the move to suburbia. In *Anatomy of a Metropolis,* Hoover and Vernon cite the findings of their New York metropolitan study.

> Most people prefer to be able to keep up with the local Joneses and tend, therefore, to seek more or less their own level in incomes. A family with children will show a strong preference for neighbors who have children of similar ages; childless families tend to feel out of place in a child-oriented suburb. Job type, even apart from its association with income levels, also is a basis for neighborhood homogeneity. Thus "lower white-collar" people often find more in common with one another than with "upper blue-collar" people of equal income and family structure.[8]

Since the majority of families who have moved to the suburbs either came with children or with the thought of raising a family, it is clear that many of the attractions of suburbia involved the perceived advantages of the suburbs for bringing up children. Suburbia was seen as a place that offered great recreational opportunities because of its openness, its unspoiled landscape, and its clean air. It was seen as a safe place compared to the city with its juvenile gangs, its underworld elements, and its dangerous streets. High quality public education was also seen in the suburb with its modern, well-equipped schools and its bright, young teachers.

Overall, people saw a chance for their children to have more than they had. They did not want to be cramped any longer in the city. They felt they did not have enough room in their apartment and wanted separate bedrooms for the children and a private yard for them to play in.

Adults also saw a better life for themselves in the suburbs, again contrasting their expectations of suburbia with their experiences in the city. One pro-suburban writer has listed some of the features of suburbia which he believes improve the quality of living for adults.

> New mechanical contrivances in the home, the wearing of casual clothes for comfort, outdoor dining, flowers, lawns, pets, all these and many more pay psychological dividends, in the form of individual achievement, pride in ownership and workmanship, and community approval and admiration. Added to these are the social assets of more intimate associations with neighbors, pleasures of gossip and visits. The

net result is to glamorize life in the suburbs as a place of retreat from the threats and frustrations of urban living. Retreat from the frustrations of urban life, in fact, is a basic virtue of the suburbs.[9]

Some suburban critics who see little of value in suburbia are at a loss to suggest reasons why people move there. A few maintain that whatever attractions suburbia may have had existed in the early stages of the suburban movement and are no longer to be found. In other words, the decision to move to the suburbs made sense only at a particular point in time. Scott Donaldson is one of those writiers who explains the growth of suburbia along these lines.

> People moved for the following reasons: practically univer-sal car ownership, the expanding highways, availability of cheap land, cheap homes, and cheap financing after World War II, and the extension of the possibility of living in the suburbs to more Americans than would have been thought possible.[10]

These developments made it possible for many people to move to the suburbs; the actual motivation to move was the result of the "suburban mystique." The several attractions of suburbia in-volved in this mystique have already been discussed.

Those who came to suburbia had many expectations of their new environment. Their vision of suburbia was that of a quiet place full of comforts and conveniences; without the problems of the city, yet within easy reach of the city. They expected at-tractive physical surroundings and a healthy social atmosphere for themselves and their children.

Disillusionment with suburbia came quickly for many subur-banites and several soon admitted that their expectations were unrealistic. They found inadequate facilities, near-impossible transportation to and from the city, economic hardships result-ing from high taxes and spiraling prices, insufficient land plan-ning and poor governmental coordination, shrinking open space, and esthetically unattractive and wasteful property development. Let us be more explicit and delineate individually the disap-pointments that newcomers to suburbia have experienced.

William Whyte in his book, *The Exploding Metropolis,* dis-cusses many of the disappointments experienced by suburbanites. He points out that young couples soon see many problems in the suburban environment for raising children, not the least of which is the limited exposure children have there to different types of people and experiences. Older couples are also disenchanted, for with their children raised and away from home, they find that suburbia offers little for them; not even suitable living quarters for their smaller space needs. Whyte predicts that suburbanites of all ages will start moving back to the city. An excerpt from Whyte's book provides a fuller discussion of these points.

> The returnees to the city will be both older people whose children have grown and whose house is too bothersome to keep up, and also, young couples who despite the violence in many of the city streets, maintain that the city can be a better place to raise children than suburbia. In the city, they believe, the children are brought up in an environment closer to reality: it is geared to adults, not children, and unlike the one-class communities of the new suburbia, it exposes children to all kinds of people, colored, white, old and young, poor and rich.[11]

> Within ten years there is likely to be a brutal disillusionment for thousands of new suburbanites. The young married couples have been seeking an economic impossibility; they want a high level of municipal services, and they want low taxes. The country the new suburbanites sought begins to vanish as soon as the next subdivision goes up and in the exploitation of land most of the new suburbs have been repeating the errors that got the city in such a mess. The nice plans for parks and playgrounds seem to get lost; there is already a marked shortage of recreation areas and the journey to work is going to be a longer one for many people.[12]

One major disappointment that suburbanites have experienced is the difficulty of commuting back and forth to the city. Highways, expressways, and freeways become virtual parking lots during rush hours. As more lanes and second levels are built, these arteries tend to become simply wider, multi-level parking lots. What happens is that as more roadway is added, the temporary relief that occurs attracts more people to use their cars until the roads again reach their saturation point. Mass transportation as a means of commutation does not exist in many metropolitan areas. Where it does exist it is usually so antiquated, inefficient, and even dangerous as to hardly be a suitable alternative to the automobile. The improvement of mass transportation is given little priority by government bodies due to lack of support from the automobile-oriented public. John Keats comments on the false notion that people had when they decided to move to suburbia that they would be within easy reach of the city. He notes that they are now beginning to discover the hidden prices: the years wasted in commuting.[13]

Transportation problems for the suburbanite are not limited to commuting to the city. Whereas there is little public transportation connecting the suburb to the city, there is virtually none joining the various parts of suburbia to each other. The automobile must again be relied upon for traveling about within suburbia, whether for shopping, going to the movies, going to church, or even to visit friends. A second car in the family is often regarded as a necessity. For those who are too poor to have a car, this transportation dilemma can reach crisis proportions.

There are essentially two reasons for the lack of an adequate public transportation system within suburbia. Firstly, the suburb's sprawl-type of development has spread people and facilities out. A good public transportation system can only be supported when people and facilities are clustered into particular areas. Secondly, suburbia was not planned in its early stages with an eye towards building a public transportation system. Early suburbanites could get around only with the automobile. Rather than inconvenience them, roads, stores, and parking areas were built to accomodate the automobile. This all but closed off the possibility of a public transportation system. Shopping areas, for example, were not clustered close to one another, but instead were separated by seas of parking lots.

The spread-out character of suburbia has created problems beyond that of transportation. Most notably, it has made suburbia physically unattractive. Because each home is placed on an individual lot, the remaining tracts of open land eventually get divided into small lots. The suburbanite who had thought the low density of development in suburbia would give it an air of openness and even a country flavor is greatly disappointed. Two commentators recently elaborated on this disappointment in the following way.

The suburbs' promise of country life within easy reach

of the pleasures of the city has proven to be false. This unordered space is neither town nor country; behind its romantic facade, suburbia contains neither the natural order of a great estate or the man-made order of the historic city. The suburb fails to be a countryside because it is too dense and it fails to be a city because it is not dense enough, or organized enough. [14]                                     .
Neighbors remain strangers and real friends are most often quite far away, as are schools, shopping centers and other facilities. The husband suffers the necessity of long-distance commuting, but the housewife who remains behind suffers the greater pain of boredom. The housewife, or mother for whom the suburb was intended, has become its greatest victim. The men, women, and children of suburbia are never quite together and never quite alone. [15]

A well-known British critic recently wrote that the roots of the sprawl problem go back to the roots of America. Ian Nairn of the London Observer says: "Americans tend to forget that the pioneering era ended almost a century ago when the railways reached California. Land is still treated as though it were an inexpendable commodity like the buffalo. 'There'll always be more around the corner' is still the ruling principle." Nairn calls suburbia a "disintegrating landscape," an environment of "total confusion and mediocrity," a place where you can drive for "hundreds of miles without ever feeling really free of the suburban tentacles." [16]

The complaint that there is not enough of a population mix in the suburbs can be attributed to lack of planning. Mass produced houses are usually offered by developers only in a particular size and price range. Reflecting on this, John Keats has said that "housing developments do not grow out of life's conditions and needs, as a city or a country village grows." [17] Keats also observed that the lack of population diversity in the suburbs leads to conformity.

> Being segregated populations, suburbanites may have a natural tendency to conformity, but, more than any other people, they tend to look anxiously around to see what their neighbors are doing and buying. They seem to think they must have whatever anyone else has, not because they need it but because other people have it, and they seem to want very much to be part of the group. [18]

One of the big disappointments of suburbanites is the high cost of living in suburbia. There is the cost of commuting, the house payments, the car payments, and, of course, the taxes. The high taxes in suburbia are a direct result of the multiplicity of governments there. Most suburban areas have several levels and several types of government. The different levels of government include the counties, the townships, and the villages, each levying their taxes one on top of the other. The various types of government districts include school districts, park districts, and water districts. With this wide array of government bodies existing in large numbers throughout the area, suburbia is a municipal jungle. The consequence of this is that government operations and public services are handled by many different units; a wasteful, inefficient, and very costly arrangement.

Most systems of government in suburbia that worked very proficiently when the population they served was about three thousand, now are straining and groaning to meet the demands of populations up to 90,000. Often, too, there is a problem resulting from the overlapping of jurisdictions. A family, due to the location of its home, may be living under several single-function governments. The home may be in completely different districts for schools, library, police protection, fire protection, and sanitation services; and one set of rules may be a hindrance on another.

Economist William Leonard in an article entitled "Economic Aspects of Suburbanization," discussed the relationship between governmental inefficiency and high taxes in the suburbs. He further considered the influence of land zoning policies in determining a community's tax base, that is, the amount and assessment of taxable property within it.

> In many suburban areas the provisions of water or other municipal services is on a small scale and uneconomic basis. Different zoning requirements create wide variation in land-use patterns and in the tax burden, as for example, between districts with considerable industry in the tax base but few residents and districts with large populations of families with young children but little industry. Such inequality of tax burden and general rise of local property taxes have led to demands for relief on the part of taxpayers. [19]

Aside from differential tax bases, the fact is that all suburban communities pay a high cost for the services they receive. This is due as much perhaps to poor planning as it is to governmental inefficiency. Public services often have not kept up with the pace of dramatic population growth. The population has multiplied up to a hundred times in some cases. This has caught governments by surprise and they have strained to provide the needed increase in services. Sewer lines, schools, libraries, police forces, and fire departments have to be greatly expanded, and in some cases developed from scratch. Developing these things requires a great deal of time and money. In an effort to pay for the necessary services and facilities, local areas have no other choice but to raise taxes, primarily property taxes. Since many suburbanites choose their suburban communities by its reputation for "low taxes," they are really shocked when the taxes begin to rise. Some area's taxes have climbed so high that they have resulted in "taxpayers' revolts." [20]

The institution most affected by local tax revolts is the school system. Since the school budget is usually the only taxation people can actually vote upon, the taxpayer takes out his hostilities at the polls. The results speak for themselves. The bills to build schools, purchase new materials, supply more buses, or enlarge school staffs have had little chance of passing. Such a problem occurred in Nassau County, New York, in 1968, when 25 out of 56 school budgets were rejected by the voters. [21] As money appropriations for the schools are blocked by the voters, the quality of education declines. This comes as a major disappointment to suburbanites who were attracted to suburbia because of the superior school systems they thought they would find there. With strained budgets, schools institute double sessions. They also curtail teacher salaries to the point where they have difficulty attracting good teachers.

Many of those who came to suburbia were also disappointed to learn that crime and juvenile delinquency were by no means absent there. Professional criminals are said to be increasingly drawn to the suburbs by it's vulnerability to be criminalized. [22] A few years ago the Federal Bureau of Investigation surprised many people in the United States by announcing that the crime rate had increased six times faster in the country's suburbs than in America's central cities. An even more dramatic fact is that more than half of the crimes in the suburbs were commited by teenagers under eighteen years of age. Local officials state that they are very concerned with the rise of organized crime. Suburban police forces are usually less well-equipped with the manpower and up-to-date equipment and training needed to deal with professional crime than are the city police departments.

Thus far in this chapter we have considered the attractions of suburbia and the later disappointments that people experienced upon moving there. We have quoted many suburban critics. It should be pointed out that there are many writers who have defended suburbia. Most of their books and articles appeared in the 1960s. Let us consider some of the comments of these pro-suburban authors.

One of these writers is Maurice Stein. He states that, "There is no reason to assume that the problems of identity, diffusion, and foreclosure described, stop at the boundary of the suburb. Role conflicts of suburbanites in which elemental human identities and problems are distorted by the quest for status are by no means their exclusive prerogative."[23] To support this view he refers to a study of a rural area by Vidich and Bensman who found these same factors at work in, of all places, the small town.[24]

William Dobriner, meanwhile, suggests that the concern with materialistic display that has been attributed to the suburbs may not be true but appears so only because the suburbs are more open than the city and therefore the possessions that people have are more apparent. He explains: "The suburbs are more open and spacious in comparison to cities and because of that life in the suburb is more visible. The visibility principle is a characteristic suburban feature."[25]

Another pro-suburban writer, Scott Donaldson, defends the suburbs by saying that most people who move there have unrealistically high expectations of suburbia.

> The disillusionment of the critics is being experienced by new suburban residents who made the move from the city to the suburb because "they thought moving out of the city would solve all their problems." Living in the suburbs didn't come up to the expectations because those expectations were too high. Helen Puner has said, "Isn't it always people, in the end, who form the character of the place they live in? And not the other way around."[26]

Herbert Gans in his book, *The Levittowners,* attacked the criticism that has been voiced that suburbia changes the people who move there — that it makes them more materialistic, more status conscious, and less individualistic. He says that people bring to suburbia attitudes and institutions and these are merely transplanted in suburbia. Because most of the people who come to suburbia are members of the middle class, it is only logical that suburbia would become a stronghold of middle class values, traditions, and life styles. Gans states this as follows:

> Choices on how to live "are not made in a vacuum," but involve values and preferences which people bring with them. The most significant fact about the origin of a new community is that it is not new at all, but only a new physical site on which people develop conventional institutions with traditional programs. [27]

Now that some of the pro-suburban commentary has been presented, let us consider what these writers are really saying. They are saying, first of all, that suburbia does not change people's attitudes. If people are materialistic and bigoted before moving to suburbia, they will be no different after living there. They are also saying that living in the suburbs is no worse than living in the city. This is like telling a person with cancer that his situation is no worse than that of a person with an acute heart disease. Besides this, the suburbanite probably moved to suburbia (and lives there) at great expense, in order to escape the ills of the city. In this respect he is like a cancer victim who became afflicted as a result of treatment received for a heart disease.

Whether the suburbanite's lot is the same or worse than that of the city dweller, he has clearly come a long way and has spent much time and money to be disappointed. The disparity between the real and the ideal suburbia is freely admitted by most suburbanites after having experienced the inconveniences and high costs of living in suburbia. The "suburban mystique" that attracted them there has not proved to be a reality.

### NOTES

1. Stephen S. Sargent and Ronald C. Williamson, *Social Psychology*, (New York: Ronald Press, 1966), pp. 116-117.

2. William Whyte, *The Organization Man*, (Garden City, New York: Doubleday and Co., 1956).
3. J. Keats, "Compulsive Suburbia," *The Atlantic*, Vol. 205, (April, 1960), pp. 47-50.
4. Frederick Allen, "Big Change in Suburbia," *Harper's Magazine*, (June 1954), p. 22.
5. S. Chermayeff and C. Alexander, *Community and Privacy: Toward New Architecture of Humanism*, 1963. The authors are both architects, who conducted research through the Joint Center for Urban Studies of M.I.T. and Harvard.
6. Raymond McKee, *Suburbs*, (Boston: Houghton Mifflin, 1957), pp. 132-133.
7. "Suburbia The Target Area," *Wilson Library Bulletin*, (October, 1966), p. 173.
8. Edgar Hoover and Raymond Vernon, *Anatomy of a Metropolis*, (Garden City, New York: Doubleday and Co., 1959), p. 100.
9. E. Mowrer, "The Family in Suburbia," *The Suburban Community*, ed. William Dobriner, (New York: Putnam, 1958), pp. 149-161.
10. Scott Donaldson, *The Suburban Myth*, (New York: Columbia University Press, 1969), pp. 154-155.
11. Whyte, *op. cit.*, p. 18.
12. *Ibid.*, p. 30.
13. Keats, *op. cit.*, p. 47.
14. Chermayeff, *op. cit.*, p. 63.
15. *Ibid.*, p. 61.
16. "Feud Between City and Suburb," *Life*, Vol. 61, (July 1, 1966), p. 63.
17. Keats, *op. cit.*, p. 48.
18. *Ibid.*, pp. 48-49.
19. In Dobriner, *op. cit.*, pp. 188-194.
20. "City and Suburbs: More and More of the Same Problem," *Time*, (December 27, 1968), p. 81.
21. "What's Wrong (And Right) With Our Suburbs?," *Senior Scholastic*, Vol. 92, (February 8, 1968), p. 6.
22. J.R. Moskin, "Suburbs: Made to Order For Crime," *Look*, Vol. 30, (May 31, 1966), p. 24.
23. Maurice Stein, *The Eclipse of Community*, (Princeton, New Jersey: Princeton University Press, 1960), p. 288.
24. Arthur J. Vidich and Joseph Bensman, *Small Town in Mass Society*, (Princeton, New Jersey: Princeton University Press, 1958).
25. William Dobriner, *Class in Suburbia*, (Englewood Cliffs, New Jersey: Prentice-Hall, 1963), p. 28.
26. Donaldson, *op. cit.*, p. 15.
27. Herbert J. Gans, *The Levittowners*, (New York: Pantheon, 1967), p. 1.

# 6

# SOCIAL PROBLEMS
# IN THE SUBURBS

There are many varieties of suburbs. They include the upper-income, the middle-income, and the lower-income communities as well as the business and industrial suburbs. Most are white, some are black, and almost none are integrated. Although each has its unique problems, some general problems affect all suburbias. These problems, however, have a different effect on various population segments. These are the problems of the young, the old, the undereducated, and the unskilled in suburbia.

There is a lack of public transportation within suburban communities and a lack of communication as well. The upper class knows little of the lower class and the young and the old do not know each other at all. Young people have their own activities and old people are shut away from society in nursing homes and isolated areas. This isolation of both groups gives individuals a distorted view of life in the formative years and in the later idle years. There is also a malalignment of people and jobs in the suburbs. This is particularly true for the unskilled who live in communities that are well-separated from employment centers.

Suburbia was originally considered to be a utopia for the young, at least for young couples with children to raise. After World War II, these young couples flocked to suburbia because it offered them the American dream of a home of their own, open spaces, clean air, better schools, and lack of traffic and congestion. It was viewed as an ideal place to raise children. For very young children this was somewhat true. The suburban problems did not emerge until these youngsters became adolescents. The teenagers were the first to sense the inadequacies of suburbia. Life in the suburbs was limited and dull to young people who were anxious to experiment and explore the world. For the parents, suburbia offered a comfortable life with many fringe benefits.

Adults move to suburbia to provide their families with suburbia's cultural advantages. The youth of today enjoys advantages that many parents growing up during the Depression and World War II were denied. It was believed after the War that by exposing children to the cultural and material advantages of the suburbs and providing them with almost unlimited opportunities for self-development, they would mature into relatively problem-free adults. The advantages of suburbia were apparent, the disadvantages less obvious. It is clear today that suburbia is not the utopia it was once thought to be. The modern youth has not emerged from suburbia problem-free. In current studies he is often pictured as "either consumed by self-pity or alienated into withdrawal from society." It is also said that, "some suburban youngsters are in flight from their own lives; others are deeply worried about what the future holds for them; and some are in revolt against their parent's suburban values."[1]

The suburban parents' concern for cleanliness, niceness, and tidiness is being answered by the youths' disinterest in such things. "Dirt, drugs and various dangers do not begin to get at the vital change in the life of America's young people that has taken place in the last two years," comments one observer.[2] The suburban emphasis on material possessions is apparently being rejected by the young.

The youth of suburbia has also been characterized as. isolated from other groups of people. "Too many of the suburbs," according to one source, "have become compounds which,

even though they are not protected by the barbed wire of
their military counterparts in occupied territories, nevertheless
set their inhabitants apart from the outside world."[3] There
is little intermingling between suburban groups. Each town or
village is a complete unit unto itself. It is quite possible for a
suburban child to grow up without venturing into nearby communities or becoming acquainted with youths from minority
groups. Youngsters from these "enclaves of affluence" experience what educator Alice Miel calls a "fragmentation of living,
with each of the enclaves becoming increasingly isolated from
the problems of all the others."[4] Lack of public transportation
is the most obvious reason for this isolation. Suburban youths,
too young to drive or unable to afford a car, find it difficult
to travel throughout suburbia. Miel points to another factor in
this: "Our nation's suburbias are evidently becoming so segregated that children can grow up without genuine contact with
others of different racial, religious or social backgrounds."[5]

The consequences of this isolation are limited experiences and
insights for the young. As Miel notes: "Suburbia's children
are living and learning in a land of distorted values and faulty
perceptions. They have only the slightest notions of others; they
judge them on the basis of suburban standards (such as 'cleanliness' and 'niceness'), generalize about groups on the basis of the
few they might have known, and think in stereotypes."[6]

There are several recorded incidents that reflect the limited
exposure of suburban youngsters. A seventeen-year-old girl from
a wealthy family was taken to lunch at a downtown department
store and did not know how to get on an escalator; she had
never seen one. A normally happy thirteen-year-old girl in one
of her rare excursions into the confusion of the inner city
broke into tears at the unaccustomed sight of an inebriated pas-
serby. A lone black child in a nursery school was getting along
well, but the parents of the white children were constantly
embarrassed because their youngsters kept insisting that the
child's mother must be the family maid. An eighth-grade boy
told his teacher, "with your talent why aren't you out in another
position making some money?"[7] Very common is the newspaper
boy who in bad weather is driven over his rounds by Mom or
Dad in the new family car. Finally, a four-year-old boy was
taken by his mother to the city where he spotted a small black
boy and said, "Look how dirty that boy's face is!"[8]

For a suburban youngster more so than a city youth experience comes filtered and preordered. The range of experience
has been preselected and highly narrowed.

If suburban children have limited learning experiences living
in suburbia, does the school system of the suburbs compensate
for this? It appears not. Alice Miel did extensive research to
determine what is being taught about human differences in suburban schools. She came up with some alarming findings, among
them: "The typical suburban elementary student's life is isolated
and circumscribed; suburban youths learn to be bigoted and
hypocritical about racial, religious, economic and ethnic differences at an early age; group predjudices take root early;
false values, materialism and anxiety are common characteristics." [9]

One of the problems of suburbia, as noted, is that there is
a disproportionately small minority population there. According
to the U.S. Census Bureau, only five percent of black Americans
live in the suburbs.[10] For the most part, these blacks live in
segregated suburban slum areas. Some of the middle-class blacks
live in integrated areas between black and white communities,
the so-called fringe zones.

The middle-class black family came to the suburbs in search
of the same suburban dream as the whites; more space, better
schools, and a home of their own. *Newsday*, a major Long Island newspaper, did a feature story on the middle-class black
family and concluded: "There really is no difference between
the average middle-class white and black family. Their values
are about the same." [11] The only difference is black families
have not been able to enjoy the same freedom of choice. Black
people are still not able to live where they desire. This situation
has a particularly great effect on the black young of suburbia
who witness the inequalities that exist in the suburban world.

Though values and aspirations may be similar, life in suburbia
is indeed different for blacks than for whites. Despite high
taxes, the black faces more severe problems in maintaining quality schools in their communities. Large influxes of welfare recipients into the black communities strain the schools by increasing the enrollment beyond capacity. At the same time, the educational needs of black children seem greater than those of
white children. *Newsday* recently reported:

These youngsters have been shortchanged by their environments and require special services in the schools. They have the same problems as other kids, but they seem to have them in greater quantity and in more intense varieties. The crux of the problem stems from the inability of the small community with limited resources to meet this sudden demand for services.[12]

Black families, particularly those with small incomes, often find themselves in homes that are poorly constructed with inadequate heating and sanitary facilities. Welfare families find landlords reluctant to repair breakdowns, thereby furthering the process of decay in the area. The youths in these areas typically exhibit disillusionment and apathy at an early age.

Little has been done to improve the situation of the suburban poor. Suburbanites appear apathetic to them, often not even admitting that they exist. A politician in Nassau County, Long Island, recently distributed a campaign brochure showing a little girl in one picture playing in a litter-strewn city lot and in another picture happily playing on a seesaw in a well-kept suburban park. It is interesting that at the time, a $100,000 federal study was being completed on the problems of the poor and the several slum communities in Nassau County. More interesting is that when the report was released, it was called a waste of money by most political figures there. In a subsequent *Newsday* editorial, it was noted that while people regard as wasteful spending money to look into the problems of poverty, they did not protest the use of over one million dollars to fight jet noise from nearby New York City airports.[13]

Another example of suburban apathy is a suburban renewal project that was launched in the suburban community of Long Beach, New York, 15 years ago. The clearance of slum housing was performed quickly, but the new housing that was planned has never been built. The only thing to rise on the site to date is a city hall.[14]

A particularly severe problem for low-income people is the physical separation from employment and recreation opportunities. Because of the lack of sufficient money to buy a car and the absence of a public transportation system in suburbia, these people find it difficult to travel to jobs and public facilities in the suburbs. Jobs are often only available far from home, making them difficult to locate and even more difficult to maintain.

As noted previously, the tax burden is a heavy one for home-owners in suburbia. The increase in population sends taxes high. The tax base (total assessment of all properties) varies from town to town so that, while taxes are high everywhere, they may be extremely high in one town and only moderately high in another. Suburban governments are attempting to lure light industry into towns as a means of keeping taxes down. The governments of suburbia have problems when they give more public services than they receive the money to pay for in taxes. The more homes and people in a town, the more services the government must supply. In the wealthier areas, the governments receive high taxes and give a minimum amount of services in return because of a lesser concentration of development and a lower population. According to Robert Wood, "If the total taxable value is greater, compared to the services required, the higher a community climbs up the scale of residential quality. The suburban governments of better class neighborhoods find themselves in the happy position of being able to receive tax returns considerably in excess of the cost of services they must render."[15] The less affluent communities find themselves in the reverse situation, as Wood points out. "Without the cushion which high site values give, the suburban government is forced to increase the tax rate as high as possible or to cut services."[16] One of the first things to be cut is usually the school budget.

The quality of suburban schools is a much debated subject. Few disagree that the wealthier areas have the better schools. In a recent newspaper series on suburban schools, statistics were presented to show that the wealthier districts had fewer drop-outs, sent more students to college, and had higher reading and mathematics proficiency ratings.[17] The poorer districts, with a higher proportion of welfare recipients and impoverished families, had a greater number and variety of special problems that require special teachers and special services. Rather than increasing services, the poor financial situation of these districts usually required them to increase class size and to cut out special programs.

The suburban high school student in most areas is placed in one of three tracks in school; the fast track (advanced curriculum), the average track (standard curriculum), or the lower track ("general" curriculum). For the student placed in the fast track, school is a positive experience. These students usually go on to college to prepare for a prestige profession. Students placed in the bottom track, meanwhile, often find school a defeating experience. These students sense their inadequacies. They comprise the potential dropouts whom the schools have failed. Suburban schools are college-oriented, and those who do not go on to college are viewed as failures. This sense of failure weighs heavily on youngsters. Employment opportunities are very limited for persons lacking education or skills. This is a major factor in suburban unemployment along with lack of transportation to available jobs. Another factor working against the poorly educated is the lack of sophistication about job hunting. In the black suburbs unemployment is almost double the level in the white suburbs. Because of a high dropout rate in the black suburbs, many unemployed youths lack even the most basic skills. It has been estimated that about half of the unemployed youth here (ages sixteen to twenty-one) are functionally illiterate.[18]

Lack of recreational facilities has proved a major problem for suburban youth. While playgrounds and ball parks are provided for the very young, the teenager often finds very little to do in suburbia. This is one of Herbert Gans' few major criticisms of suburbia. "Many consider it a dull place to which they have been brought involuntarily by their parents. Often there is no place to go and nothing to do after school."[19] Lack of facilities and athletic programs are the most common complaints of suburban teenagers. There are few facilities that are available for young people throughout the year, especially night-time facilities. In many communities this fact has been ignored and the local movie house, bowling alley, or pizza place is expected to take up the slack and energies of the adolescent.[20] If the individual is old enough he may be permitted to the "local tavern" and may soon make this the center of his social life.

There is the constant inconvenience and problem of trying first to figure out where to go, then how to get there, and finally by what means to get back home again. Physical mobility is a major problem in suburbia for young people. One of the biggest inadequacies of the suburbs is the lack of a public transportation system, making suburbia a car-oriented society. Owning a car is a necessity if one wishes to travel throughout suburbia. For the young who cannot have a car, hitchhiking or using parents as chauffeurs are alternatives. Suburbia is designed for adults, not teenagers. The generation gap between teenagers and parents is clearly fostered by suburbia.

Juvenile delinquency and illegal drug use are suburban problems that can be partly attributed to boredom. Statistics on juvenile delinquency reflect the high incidence of crime among the young. Of all persons arrested in 1965, for example, about twenty percent were under eighteen and about thirty percent were under twenty-one. Eleven- to seventeen-year olds, although they represent only thirteen percent of the population, were responsible for half the arrests for property crimes—burglary, larceny, and motor vehicle theft.[21] Statistics on youth offenses still show a higher rate in suburban slums than in other areas of suburbia, but this is misleading. Many of the upper and middle class youth offenses do not reach the police or the courts. But crime experts who have studied suburbia conclude: "Crime in the cities is largely the work of the poor but in the suburbs most of it is committed by the well-to-do." [22]

Besides boredom, there are other factors that prompt suburban youth to commit crimes. Studies of criminals from middle- and upper-income families show, for example, that often "the privileges of wealth breed contempt for the rights of others and a sense of superiority which takes the form of self-indulgence." [23] It is claimed that this is more common in suburbs than among similarly advantaged youths of the city, perhaps because suburbanites are more likely to get away with it. Suburban police have smaller forces than urban police and they have been found to have "a more respectful attitude toward the public they guard." [24] Also, the urban youth looking for unusual activities can find them in the city. It is easier for him to rebel there without actually becoming a rebel.

Illegal drug use in suburbia has been becoming increasingly widespread in recent years. Such drugs as marijuana and LSD are particularly common. Why are youths so attracted to drugs in view of the physical and legal dangers of using them? Leonard Wolf in "The Making of a Hippie," points out:

> The answer is that the dangers have a symbolic value: they can be risked alone; they can say no to their parents, to society, to the bleak future. But more than that, the dangers can be associated with heroic explorations. If America has room for only a handful of astronauts, if the world has only one Everest and it has already been climbed, then

there are left the interior horizons, the howling tundras of the mind or clear places of dazzling illumination where God or lightning may be expected to speak.[25]

The use of drugs in suburban high schools and colleges is reportedly reaching large proportions, but accurate statistics are impossible to obtain. Police have spoken of their frustrations in attempting to determine how many young people are currently using drugs. Parents seek private solutions for their children's drug problems. School administrators conceal incidents of drug use.

One problem experienced by the young person in the suburbs is the fact that working parents are absent for a major portion of the time. This is because it is often necessary to commute long distances to the city. The time devoted to commuting usually varies anywhere from two to six hours each day. The working parent or parents leave the home as early as six or seven o'clock in the morning and return as late as seven or eight at night. This removes an authority figure from the home for much of the time and seriously limits the guidance and counseling available to the child.

Obviously, there are many conditions in suburbia that affect the young and cause problems for them. Elderly persons form another group that is also disadvantaged by the suburban environment.

In a recent issue of *Aging,* it was reported: "It is a modern tragedy that the role of older people is diminishing and that society has given them less and less to do with their added years." [26] Retirement, generally assumed to be a time for older people to relax and enjoy life, is often filled with problems. The main problem facing the elderly in suburbia is housing. Where to live and with whom is a major decision for the elderly (when they have a choice), because it determines largely how contentedly they will spend their last years. Many married couples choose to keep their homes and live alone. This usually works out well if their married children live nearby. Widows and widowers, if they choose to live alone, face more problems than a married couple. The elderly need someone to visit them and take care of their special needs. Elderly people living alone also face the problem of isolation. Because of their inability to travel easily, they run the risk of losing contact with the outside world. Their isolation is due not only to lack of transportation, but to the very design of suburban areas with their freeways, throughways, and expressways that separate areas. It is noteworthy that a high proportion of pedestrian deaths occur among the elderly.[27]

Regarding their care, the elderly need regular medical treatment and nutritional meals. Often they are undernourished because of lack of money or inability to shop and prepare meals. The elderly are in need of services that are often not available to them. Many have limited financial resources, which places some services beyond their reach—if the services exist at all. Many of the services offered by communities are only available when requested by letter or application, and many of the elderly simply do not know how to go about enlisting these services. Most communities do not recognize the uniqueness of each elderly individual and do not try to evaluate each one's individual needs. On this subject *Aging* reports: "The failure has been the lack of specific goals to ameliorate specific conditions relating to aging and failure to design services to dignify and ennoble the human spirit and condition."[28]

The elderly black person faces a particularly difficult time in old age. Blacks often experience an old age of poverty with little chance of work. Opportunities to live in good housing are also extremely limited for them. Because of lack of income they are usually forced to live in deteriorated houses or apartments in areas with a high proportion of robberies and break-ins.[29] Fifty percent of all elderly blacks live on less than $2000 a year, according to the Social Security Administration. The blacks face the same problems of isolation, transportation, and limited services as the whites, but they must endure more severe housing and financial problems due to discrimination and other factors.

In an attempt to grapple with the problem of isolation, many elderly people become involved in senior citizens groups. A few suburban areas have senior centers where volunteers provide homemaker and protective service, counseling, and friendly visiting.[30] But many senior citizens do not know about these centers, while others who do know cannot travel to them. In most suburban communities, moreover, these facilities are simply not available.

Limited income is making retirement difficult for many suburban residents. Besides having low retirement incomes, they have the added problem of these incomes being fixed, while suburban living costs are constantly rising. Social security and pensions do not always provide enough income. It is a myth that living in the city is more costly than living in the suburbs. This myth seems to have arisen because of the large number of tourists who get bilked in the city and because of the several speciality shops with high-priced merchandise located there. But the fact of the matter is that the cost of food, clothing, transportation, and basic household supplies is higher in the suburbs. A recent study of suburban Suffolk County on Long Island reported that food costs there averaged five percent higher than in New York City while clothing rates were ten percent higher.[31] Even if older people are able to complement their income with a small job, there is still the problem of finding a means to get to the job location.[32] Most require public transportation which is largely unavailable. Financially, many cannot possibly afford the costs of a car on their limited funds.[33] Others, meanwhile, turn in their driver's license when they realize their reflexes are not as quick nor are they as alert as they used to be.[34] They are at the mercy of the limited public transportation facilities.

The several social and economic problems imposed by suburbia on its older citizens causes many of these people to move back to the city. This trend of people moving back to the city is sometimes viewed as being due to an attraction that the city has in later years, when in fact it is the result of rejection by suburbia.

In addition to the young and old, there is another group of suburban residents that is especially disadvantaged by suburbia. This group is the uneducated and unskilled. For them life in the suburbs is filled with problems. Many uneducated and unskilled lack the knowledge and sophistication to find a job in suburbia, where employers are spread out and located often in out-of-the-way places. Government employment assistance is usually limited to a particular town or county. Another problem is that if an individual is poorly educated and cannot read properly he will not be able to obtain any type of job except the most menial. Lack of a skill similarly results in limited job opportunity.

Unemployment in suburbia has an ironic twist. There are many unskilled jobs available, but employers are finding it difficult to get workers. The main reason is the lack of transportation in suburbia, and this is where the irony lies. Residents of poverty areas are more dependent on public transportation than are people in middle-income neighborhoods, but public transportation serves them less well.[35] There is often a lack of bus routes from the poorer areas to the industrial parks where unskilled jobs are available. Car pools are sometimes organized but are not reliable because of car breakdowns and owner sicknesses. Often the expense of commuting to the work location makes up a sizable portion of the salary of the individual and may be more than the difference between wages and welfare payments. In most instances the unskilled do not receive wages beyond the established minimum. Another problem is that in the suburbs there are very limited living accommodations within the financial means of the unskilled.

Facilities that are equipped to handle the problem of educating groups with the basics that are required for initial entry and upgrading in a job are largely absent in the suburbs. The reason for this is that there has been relatively little public pressure for any type of educational program outside of the regular school curriculum designed to provide education to children. Basic education for adults has been overlooked in most communities.

An added problem of the uneducated in suburbia is keeping abreast of what goes on in the suburban community. The suburbs are a massive sprawl of land and people. News from the mass media is geared mainly to the central cities. Without information and informative communication, there is difficulty understanding the problems close at hand. Because of this, the uneducated in suburbia can very easily turn into social isolates.

Because the suburbs have been set up basically for family-oriented groups, there is a definite problem that has arisen regarding the single-person household in suburbia. In most instances the unmarried adult finds it difficult to associate and communicate with other inhabitants of the suburban community. There are many uncomfortable situations for a single person in a couple-oriented community. Opportunities are few for singles between the ages of 25 and 40 to meet and socialize in the suburbs. There are also limited public services and facilities especially geared to single people.

Suburbia is a series of communities and population groups that exist independently of one another. There is little intermingling, interaction, and communication between them.

Isolation is a common suburban problem. It exists everywhere and affects almost everyone. Classes and cultural groups do not mix in suburbia. The upper and middle classes know little or nothing of the poor black families a few miles away. White apathy and indifference to the problems of poverty are widespread throughout suburbia. Suburban schools are geared to the college bound middle class youth and tend to discriminate against the poor minorities.

The young of suburbia are affected by this isolation. They are growing up without seeing or knowing anyone different from themselves. They have taken their material position for granted and suffer from boredom and a lack of goals. Juvenile delinquency and drug use is widespread in the higher-income areas.

The older residents of suburbia suffer from isolation too. They live apart from society in their own groups. They find it difficult traveling about suburbia and are hard pressed to meet the rising costs of living there on their fixed income. Many have lost interest in the activities of the world.

Poor public transportation is a major problem which helps to foster isolation. The young, old, and poor find it difficult to travel throughout suburbia. It affects the poor economically because they cannot always afford a car and must therefore rely on public transportation to get to work. What little transportation is available is geared more to the middle class than the lower class. Because suburbia is sprawled out over a large area, jobs are often far from the poor districts that have the most unemployment and the greatest need for the jobs.

Suburbia was conceived as a residential area for white middle and upper class young couples with children to raise. The major social problems of suburbia affect anyone who does not fit into this mold — the young, the old, the black, the poor, the uneducated, the unskilled, and the unmarried.

NOTES

1. James A. Meyer, *Suburbia: A Wasteland of Disadvantaged Youth*, p. 575.
2. Leonard Wolf, "The Making of a Hippie," *PTA Magazine*, (January, 1969), p. 5.
3. Alice Miel, "The Shortchanged Children of Suburbia," Institute of Human Relations Press, (1967), p. 5.
4. *Ibid.*, p. 5.
5. Meyer, *op. cit.*, p. 575.
6. *Ibid.*

7. Peter Wyden, "Suburbia's Coddled Kids," *Saturday Evening Post*, Vol. 233, (October 8, 1960), pp. 34-35.
8. Theodore M. Newcomb, *Readings in Social Psychology*, (New York: 1958), pp. 342-343.
9. Miel, *op. cit.*
10. "Can the Suburbs Be Opened," *Time*, (April 6, 1970), p. 53.
11. "What do the Middle Class Blacks Want? Only What Whites Want." *Newsday*, (April 29, 1970), p. 7.
12. *Ibid.*
13. "Caso's Complaint," *Newsday*, (November 20, 1969), p. 1b.
14. "Where's the Renewal?" *Newsday*, (May 17, 1969), p. 14.
15. Robert C. Wood, *Suburbia: Its People and Their Politics*, (Boston: Houghton Mifflin, 1958), p. 213.
16. *Ibid.*, p. 214.
17. Martin Buskin, "School Statistics: A Numbers Game?" *Newsday*, (March 27, 1970).
18. James E. Allen, Jr. "The Right to Read — Target For the 1970's," *PTA Magazine*, (December, 1969), p. 7.
19. Herbert J. Gans, *The Levittowners*, (New York: Pantheon, 1967), p. 206.
20. Walter McKain, Jr., "Rural Suburbs and Their People," *Journal of Co-operative Extension*, Vol. 1, No. 2, (Summer, 1963), p. 77.
21. Vernon Lynn, "What We Don't Know About Delinquency," *PTA Magazine*, (June, 1969), p. 5.
22. David Loth, *Crime in the Suburbs*, p. 11.
23. *Ibid.*, p. 28.
24. *Ibid.*, p. 29.
25. Wolf, *op. cit.*, p. 8.
26. "Plight of Older People in Urban Areas," *Aging*, (February, 1969), p. 10.
27. *Ibid.*
28. "Help for the Aged." *Aging*, (February-March, 1970), p. 9.
29. "Old and Black," *Harvest Years*, (November, 1969), p. 38.
30. Howard Whitman, *A Brighter Later Life*, (Englewood Cliffs, New Jersey: Prentice-Hall, 1961).
31. "Suffolk Prices Top the City's," *Newsday*, (August 23, 1969), p. 7.
32. Albert J. Reiss, et al., *Occupations and Social Status*, (New York: The Free Press, 1962), pp. 33-34.
33. *Ibid.*, p. 49.
34. Read Bain, *Sociology Readings*, (Philadelphia: Lippincott, 1962), p. 124.
35. "You Can't Get From There to Here," *Trans-action*, (April, 1969), p. 19.

# 7

# CITY PROBLEMS AND SUBURBAN GUILT

Thus far the contemporary suburban scene has been explored and some of suburbia's problems have been examined. The conclusion was reached that suburbia functions in such a way as to breed many problems for those living there. Certain groups of suburbanites, notably the young, the old, the poor, and the unskilled, are particularly disadvantaged by suburbia.

The ills fostered by the suburbs extend beyond suburbia. In large measure many of the problems of the cities can be directly attributed to the suburbs, for suburbia has helped to bring about the economic crisis, the jobless situation, the deterioration of public services, and the perpetuation of ghettoes in cities. It has helped to do this by drawing the affluent from the city, by excluding the city's poor, by pulling industry out of the city, by discriminating against black people, and by diverting federal and state funds from the city.

Few disagree that cities have been on the decline and that their problems are severe. David Rockefeller, president of New

York's Chase Manhattan Bank, recently went down the list of the major ills of urban areas. He identified the major ones as inadequate educational systems, hard-core unemployment, hazardous pollution of natural resources, antiquated transportation, poor housing, insufficient and ineffective public facilities, lack of equal opportunity for all, and a highly dangerous failure of communication between young and old, and between black and white. To these conditions he gave one overall label — the urban crisis.[1]

In general the city's problems affect black people most severely. This is because black people live largely in the city ghettoes where conditions are worse. The black population of the cities were left behind during the mass migration to suburbia. This occurred because most of them happened to be poor and all of them happened to be black. Their low economic status excluded them from the middle- and upper-income housing characteristic of suburbia. Their skin color, meanwhile, made them an easily identifiable target for discrimination and exclusion from suburban neighborhoods.

The suburban migration is actually the last of three migrations that have affected the situation of black people in this country. The first migratory movement involved the relocation of rural people to the cities. This took place after the Civil War and consisted, for the most part, of people moving from the rural South to the industrial North. Many of these people were black. Measures taken to restrain black movement varied. Racial zoning was among the first. The supposition was that this was authorized by the "separate but equal" doctrine as well as by the best principles of safe and sound city development.[2]

The second migration was the migration of people to America from foreign countries. This migration occurred in various stages; first the Irish and German, then the Oriental, later the Italian and Slav, and finally the Puerto Rican. The most intensive period was from 1870 to 1924. As these immigrants arrived in the cities they took over many of the jobs held by blacks who were already there. They began by immediately replacing blacks in many of the menial jobs they held, but there were some jobs held by already established blacks for which these new immigrants could not qualify. The blacks were cooks, waiters, barbers, coachmen, butlers, footmen, and general household servants. But even this situation began to change by the eve of World War I as noted by Frank Warne, a writer of the period, who reported:

> Today, all these and many other positions have been wrested from the Negro by Slav and Italian. Our shoes are now blacked by the Greek and Italian, they wait upon us at tables in our hotels and restaurants; we are shaved by the Italian barber; this newer immigrant is cooking our food and doing our household work, as the women of these races in ever increasing number join the men who preceded them. What has become of the Negroes they have supplanted is a serious question. As a general thing, not only has his economic status been lowered but he has also been removed from the close social intercourse with the white race which these occupations brought to him.[3]

The motivation of foreign immigrants to leave their native land and come to America was based upon several factors. Charles Abrams states these as follows: "The immigrants came for different reasons — land hunger and food hunger; insect plague and human plague; political persecution; the lure of gold and the ballyhoo of steamship agents; overpopulation and starvation; crop failure; displacement through mechanization or the competition of female and child labor."[4] It is ironical that the very ills from which these people fled in foreign countries, they helped create in America to the detriment black citizens. Only the economic optimism of the 1920's slackened the move toward racism.[5] Foreigners migrated to this country by the millions each year until 1924 when the McCarran-Walter Act was passed, establishing a quota system that sharply limited the number of people allowed into this country each year.

Last of the major migrations was the mass movement to suburbia. This really got underway after World War II and has continued to the present. Those involved in this migration have been mostly white city dwellers who have sought to escape city conditions, while at the same time retaining their good city jobs. Most of these people have equated city problems with the large concentration of black people living there. They have therefore worked hard to keep suburbia "lily white." Of course, most black city dwellers could not move to suburbia anyway since builders have erected homes beyond their purchasing means. But those who could afford to move have been systematically discriminated against. As the suburban movement continued, fewer and fewer whites were being left in the city and the proportion of blacks there grew. Many cities soon had black majorities. This became a vicious cycle, since the motivation of white people to move became greater as the white population decreased. When some of the remaining whites left, it decreased the white population even further. By 1966, as a result of the suburbanization of the white population, only 42 percent of non-rural whites remained in cities. Among non-whites, on the other hand, more than 82 percent lived in central cities in 1966 — a much higher proportion than in 1950.

The racial discrimination that has been practiced by suburbanites could have been anticipated in view of the tradition of racism in America. From the beginning, federal laws and Supreme Court decisions discriminated against blacks. The Dred Scott Decision (1857), for example, stated that Negroes were not citizens, that they were inferior to whites, that they had no rights which a white man was bound to respect, and that they were not and could not become part of the American people, even when accorded the right to vote. Another example is the Constitution of the United States. The first and fourth articles of the Constitution speak for themselves. Article One labeled the black slave as being worth three-fifths of a white man and ruled that blacks should be discounted in this way for purposes of congressional representation. Article Four sought to reinforce the institution of slavery by stating that a slave who escapes to another state could not obtain sanctuary there, even if it barred slavery, and that he must be returned to his owner.

Suburbia has discriminated against the poor, and therefore, the blacks in various ways. Some of the devices used have been minimum lot-size requirements, minimum house-size requirements, restrictive subdivision regulations, and unduly expensive building standards. In addition to these devices, many suburban communities have adopted zoning ordinances that prohibit development of all forms of multi-family housing.

Occasionally, a large township within suburbia will propose that some multi-family housing should be built within it. But the many incorporated villages in the township usually prohibit it with their own zoning. The township of Islip on Long Island recently planned a town-house and high-rise condominium project in an area of the town known as Great River that was not incorporated as a village. The residents here quickly filed petition for incorporation to become a village and block the move.

Restrictive zoning is occasionally tested in court and usually emerges victorious. Certain villages in Nassau County, New York recently introduced zoning that required a person to own five acres of land before he could build a house. The courts ruled that this was valid in order to help preserve the "character" of the area. To guarantee that the courts will uphold restrictive zoning, many towns and villages have commissioned master plans which are used as evidence in court. The town of Southampton in Suffolk County, New York, is now having a master plan completed. One of the approaches of the planners involves a projection that the town's water supply is enough for only a small population and, on the basis of this, restrictive zoning will probably be recommended.

There are a few recent examples of the courts overturning restrictive zoning. In the court case of Lakeland Bluff, the Appellate Court of Illinois ruled that it was unreasonable for the county to prevent the plaintiff from developing a trailer park on his land. The land was located in the middle of a large area which had been strip-mined for coal and subsequently abandoned. It was described by the court as "broken up into mounds, water holes and small lakes" and "substantially useless for farming." The court also said that the trailer park would be "properly buffered" by the surrounding wastelands. Decisions of this type seem to indicate that the position of the courts is as follows: Low-income people have a constitutional right to live at high densities on the most worthless land having the worst possible environmental conditions as long as the land is "properly buffered" from any place they might possibly want to go.

Suburbanites are intent upon keeping out the poor and the black (usually equated as the same). They have several reasons for this. The suburban homeowner is afraid of losing (1) social status, (2) neighborhood associations, and (3) investment. These fears are based upon seven fallacies.

1) Negroes and whites do not mix.

2) Negroes are dirty and will spoil the neighborhood.
3) Entry of minority families into a neighborhood hurts the social prestige of the area.
4) The minority always goes where it is not wanted.
5) Once the minority establishes a beachhead, many more will soon follow and displace the once-dominant majority.
6) Property values go down wherever a minority moves into a neighborhood.
7) Homogeneity stabilizes value.

This stereotype of minorities is generally based upon the image of the slum-dweller as the one responsible for conditions in the city, rather than the other way around. The competition for dwellings has become a main factor in arousing common fears and insecurities.

One of the major reasons upper and middle class whites flee the city for the suburbs is to escape from their black neighbors. The greatest amount of bias against blacks is found in the middle class because it is into their areas that the blacks are most likely to be able to penetrate in large numbers. The upper class is so far removed from the blacks that they are convinced the blacks can never enter their sanctuary.

Actually, a number of blacks are moving to the suburbs. As one researcher has found, "Two hundred thousand middle-class blacks are moving to the suburbs each year, but white hostility tends to confine the newcomers to black suburbs."[6] While the suburbs are legally open to the blacks, the anti-discrimination housing laws are not enforced. This keeps most of the blacks in the cities' ghettos. The minority groups in the suburbs are a very small minority, as suburbia is still generally white middle class.

The predominant view among suburbanites seems to be that they should have the freedom to discriminate if they please. Harry P. Bergmann, vice-president of Washington's Riggs National Bank, spoke for many when he told the U.S. Civil Rights Commission, "People have moved to the suburbs so they could live with the people that they wanted to live with and if we are going to have integrated housing out there, they will move farther out. Is there no end to it? I mean don't we have the freedom of living where we want to and who we want to live with?"[7]

The black and the poor, by being kept out of the suburbs, are being denied opportunities for living improvement and for educational and economic advancement. This is because the suburbs can have much to offer the low-educated, low-income person. The relationship between place of residence and opportunity has long been recognized. In its December 1968 report, the President's Committee on Urban Housing (Kaiser Commission) concluded that:

> The location of one's place of residence determines the accessibility and quality of many everyday advantages taken for granted by the mainstream of American society. Among these commonplace advantages are public educational facilities for a family's children, adequate police and fire protection, and a decent surrounding environment. In any case, a family should have the choice of living as close as economically possible to the breadwinner's place of employment. [8]

The exclusion of black people and poor people from suburbia has limited these groups largely to the slum housing for which the cities are well known. All experts agree that the housing situation in cities is deplorable. Little relief is expected in the near future. Since federal housing programs are generally shaped to encourage private enterprise, it is generally believed that there will be very little low-income building in the cities where it is needed most. It is estimated that it would cost 1.1 billion dollars a year to replace at current construction costs the abandoned apartments in New York City alone. This amount is nearly half the federal government's total housing budget for the whole nation. Meanwhile, the Federal Department of Housing and Urban Development has plans to acquire millions of acres of land outside of cities that could cost at a conservative estimate, anywhere from twenty to one hundred billion dollars. The land will be used to build town houses and middle- and upper-income apartments. The purpose of the plan is not to assure better housing for the poor but to improve patterns of land use in the suburbs. [9]

Suburbia is clearly where the newer and better housing is being built in our metropolitan regions. The private enterprise system is such that home builders are looking to suburbia for land, volume, and profits. The city, meanwhile, is being left with a housing stock that is old, deteriorated, nonfunctional, and insufficient.

At the same time that the bulk of the new housing is being built in suburbia, industry is also moving out of the cities and relocating in the suburbs. Left behind is a crisis in employment. While job opportunities have been expanding in the suburbs, they have been declining in the cities. More importantly, the jobs that the suburbs have been stealing from the cities have been those at the lower occupational levels. These types of jobs are the most severely needed in the cities since here is where the greatest concentration of low-skilled people live.

One of the most striking aspects of American economic growth over the last two decades is the fact that 80 percent of the new jobs created in the nation's large metropolitan areas have been in the suburban communities. The central cities of these metropolitan areas have not only failed to win a significant share of new urban employment, but, in some cases, they have experienced a net outflow of jobs. In the tri-state New York area, for example, the central city gained only 111,000 new jobs between 1952 and 1966, compared with a gain of 888,000 jobs for the region as a whole.[10]

Industry has been attracted to suburbia for several reasons. Changes in production methods that require spacious, single-story plants is one of the most important factors.[11] A parcel of land large enough to serve this purpose in the city is rare and very costly. With only small parcels of land available, plants are extremely expensive to build in the city because they have to be built up, rather than out, increasing construction costs enormously. In the period between 1948 and 1954, the average increase in employment in the central city area was 1.0 percent. In that same period the suburban increase was about 17 percent. In the period from 1954 to 1958 the central city increase in employment averaged 0.6 percent, while it was about 12.5 percent in suburbia. Finally, from 1958 to 1963 the central city actually decreased 0.5 percent in the percentage of employment while the suburb increased 12.0 percent.

Many suburban communities which face fiscal problems welcome factories to broaden their tax base but discourage apartment-dwelling families. Because multi-family housing is the most that many minority individuals can afford, they are excluded from suburbia. In effect, blacks and other minorities are unable to follow their jobs to the suburbs.

The December 1968 report of the National Commission on Urban Problems (Douglas Commission) considered the employment problems of ghetto residents and noted that:

> Available employment of the type for which slum adults might qualify is generally not available in the slum. In a recent year, 63 percent of all construction permits for industrial buildings were issued for locations outside central cities. On the other hand, 73 percent of office building construction permits were issued inside central cities. Central cities increasingly are becoming white-collar employment centers while the suburbs are becoming the job employment areas for new blue-collar workers. This is ironical in view of the fact that low-paid blue-collar workers, especially if they are Negroes, live in the central cities while the white-collar workers are increasingly living in the suburbs. Traveling to work becomes increasingly difficult for both.[12]

There have been various government programs aimed at reversing the trend of the suburbanization of industry and jobs, but these programs have not had the expected impact and it is doubtful that they will be any more effective in the future. While isolated examples of in-city plant location will occur, as in the case of the IBM plant in Bedford-Stuyvesant,[13] the private sector will continue to locate the bulk of its new plants and equipment outside central cities. In the same year in which IBM created 300 jobs in Bedford-Stuyvesant, the company created 3,000 jobs in the New York region as a whole. The blacks of Bedford-Stuyvesant did not have access to these 2,700 other jobs.

Similar to the reduction of employment opportunities in the city as a result of suburban development, public education has suffered in the city due to the growth in suburbia. There is little question that the suburbs have played an important part in the life of the cities regarding education. With the increase in population in the suburbs, there has been a need for major capital expenditures for school facilities. To meet this need, state and federal funds have been diverted from the urban areas to the suburbs.

Suburban schools are considered superior to urban schools. It has been noted: "Most differences between suburban and urban communities are obviously in favor of suburban schools. They typically have better qualified teachers, newer buildings and higher educational standards." [14] The higher school tax that suburbanites pay annually contributes to the better schools, but suburban schools "also ordinarily benefit more from state aid than do urban schools." [15]

Educational inequality between cities and suburbs is common in our nation today. The highest incidence of underachievement and the highest dropout rates are found in the black and Puerto Rican city ghettos. In the world of the ghetto, many of the hard-core unemployed are so lacking in education that they have to be taught even how to learn. [16] Black leaders frequently point out that blacks go to inferior schools, to get an inferior education, to get an inferior job, to be last to be hired and first to be fired, to be passed over for promotion, and to have a shorter life. [17]

Another area in which the cities have suffered at the hands of suburbia is transportation. In recent years, 235 bus and subway companies in cities have gone out of business. The remaining companies have progressively deteriorated. Today they give their riders fewer runs, older cars, and poorer service. This is the condition of urban transportation. Some of this has been caused by a decrease in passengers, which can be attributed to the flight to the suburbs. [18] The money that is sorely needed to rescue urban mass transit is going to develop suburban express-ways in order to make it easier for those who have fled the cities to commute to their jobs. In the period 1959-1969, only a fraction of the amount spent on highways was used to improve mass transit. During that period, the federal government spent $42.6 billion for highways and only $296.8 million for mass transit. In other words, for every dollar used for mass transit, about $130 was spent on highways.

Many of the problems of the cities have been examined here, and it is clear that suburbia has contributed to these problems in several ways. Yet a full study of the range of city problems that suburbia has influenced has not been attemped. For example, the question of environmental pollution of cities has not been considered. Suburbia has certainly contributed to city air pollution since automobiles, a major source of air pollution, are imported into the city each day by commuting suburbanites. Even the pollution of city rivers and streams has been traced to suburbia. In 1969 when the sludge-filled Cuyahoga River in the City of Cleveland caught fire, an investigation revealed that many of the companies dumping industrial waste into the river were located upsteam in suburban communities.[19]

The city is indeed plagued by many problems. But to think that suburbia has had nothing to do with these is simply to deny the evidence. Many city problems have been caused directly by the suburban phenomenon, while several others have been seriously aggravated by it.

## NOTES

1. "The War Business Must Win," *Business Week*, No. 2096, (November 1, 1969), p. 63.
2. Charles Abrams, *Forbidden Neighbors*, (New York: Harper and Brothers, 1951), p. 26.
3. Frank Julian Warne, *Immigration Invasion*, (New York: Dodd, Mead and Co., 1913), p. 174.
4. Abrams, *op. cit.*, p. 10.
5. *Ibid.*, p. 13.
6. "Can the Suburbs Be Opened," *Time*, (April 6, 1970), p. 53.
7. Don Oberdorfer and Milton MacKaye, "Will Negroes Crack the Suburbs?" *Saturday Evening Post*, Vol. 235, (December 22, 1962), p. 72.
8. "The Report of the President's Committee on Urban Housing," *A Decent Home*, (Washington, D.C.: GPO, 1969), p. 13.
9. "Revolution in Suburbia," *Forbes*, Vol. 105, No. 7, (April 1, 1970), pp. 24-26.
10. Paul and Linda Davidoff and Neil Newton Gold, "Suburban Action: Advocate Planning For An Open Society," *Journal of The American Institute of Planners*, Vol. 36, No. 1, (January, 1970), p. 13.
11. John F. Kain, "The Distribution and Movement of Jobs and Industry," *The Metropolitan Enigma*, ed. James Q. Wilson, (Cambridge, Massachusetts: Harvard University Press, 1968), p. 3.
12. "Report of the National Commission on Urban Problems," *Building the American City*, (Washington, D.C.: GPO, 1969), p. e.
13. Robert Schrank and Susan Stein, "Industry in the Black Community: IBM in Bedford-Stuyvesant," *Journal of the American Institute of Planners*, Vol. 35, No. 3, (September, 1969), pp. 348-51.
14. Arthur Adkins, "Inequities Between Suburban and Urban Schools," *Educational Digest*, (February, 1969), p. 50.
15. *Ibid.*, p. 51.
16. "The War That Business Must Win," *Business Week*, No. 2096, (November 1, 1969), p. 65.
17. Elliot Liebow, "No Man Can Live With the Terrible Knowledge That He is Not Needed," *New York Times*, (April 5, 1970), Section 6, p. 13.
18. "Special Report," *Business Week*, No. 2096, (November 1, 1969), p. 70.
19. "Cleveland River So Dirty It Burns," *New York Times*, (June 29, 1969).

# III

# THE FUTURE OF THE SUBURBS

# 8

# SUBURBIA IN TRANSITION

Today's suburbs are in a transitory stage. There are many features of present suburbs that differentiate them from suburbs of just a few years ago. And there are several trends under way that are likely to have substantial impact on suburbia in the future and transform it even further. These trends are occurring both within the suburbs and nationwide. Population trends, political trends, cultural trends, land development trends, technological advances in transportation and production — these are some of the ongoing developments that are causing transition in suburbia.

Presently, the nation and the world are caught up in a massive population explosion that is radically altering the face of the land. The effects that this explosion is having on the suburban situation are indeed very great, not only in terms of new construction but also in the political environment and the social structure of the suburbs.

Trends in the size of the average American family and fluctuations in birth rates are affecting the current population picture. Based on an analysis of families between 1871 and 1875, there were approximately 3.5 children per woman in the United States at that time. This figure dropped to 2.2 children per woman between 1906 and 1910. By 1955 the figure jumped up again to 3.3 children.[1] This rise was due to the post-World War II baby boom which continued right into the 1960's.[2] Another trend in population that has developed historically is the decrease in the death rate. More people live to be senior citizens today and they occupy that status longer than ever before.

The greater numbers of younger and older people have led to a tapering off of demand for home ownership because the circumstances of the younger and older age groups favor apartment living.[3] Clearly the demand for apartment dwellings in suburbia today is great and it is likely that the pressures for this type of housing will grow as the age profile continues to change.

One consequence of the huge population increase in suburbia is the deterioration of public services there. This has occurred because the uncontrolled pattern of suburban growth has precluded adequate planning. Anyone living in suburbia can attest to the fact that suburban services have not kept pace with the rapid population growth. These services include fire departments, sewage lines, schools, libraries, and other important needs, usually none of which are planned ahead of time.[4] The result is constant restructuring and redesigning, cheating the individual of quality services, while at the same time burdening him with increased taxes.

As noted previously, a suburban government structure set up to serve a community of three thousand people often does a creditable job, but when it is pressed to serve ninety thousand people or more the situation becomes severely strained.[5] Also pointed out earlier was that eratic and overlapping jurisdictional boundaries among fire districts, school districts, sanitation districts, and other districts add to the difficulty. Lack of unified planning by local governments merely compounds the already difficult and fragmented situation.

What lies ahead in population trends must be predicted and examined in the light of such factors as migration patterns and the age groups involved, replacement levels, and personal family size preferences. It is clear, first of all, that the younger and

older age groups are increasing more than the people in between.[6] Future projections indicate that households with heads
under 25 years old will increase 75 percent and those with
heads over 55 years old will go up 24 percent. But household
heads in the 25 to 54 group will increase only by 6 percent.[7]
This will very likely lead to a higher mobility rate, since child-
less people tend to be more mobile than others. Besides an
increase in mobility, another major implication is that much of
the future demand for living quarters will be for apartments.[8]
Looking to the future, a national demographer considered the
fact that if today's young couples and those people just entering
adulthood have three children per couple, the nation's population
can be expected to double in 50 years.[9] The researcher responsible for this projection suggested that an ideal "replacement level"
of two children per couple should be sought so that the soaring
population of this country could level off at 300 million people
in 25 to 35 years.[10]

But most couples concern themselves little with future genera-
tions and plan the size of their families for personal rather than
societal reasons. Some couples feel that status is increased
with a large family, while others tend to regard greater expression of love to be the product of a larger number of children.[11]
In the coming generation, the number of women of childbearing
age will double. In 1960 the women in this age group (15 to
45 years) totaled 36 million. They will increase to 54 million by
1980 and to 70 million by 1990.[12]

The population explosion can be expected to have several
effects on suburbia. For one thing, the little remaining open
space will probably have to be filled in with new development.
This land, because of its scarcity and high value, very likely
will be developed with high intensity uses. It will be the site of
office buildings, department stores, and apartment houses. Because of poor planning and poor coordination, this growth
probably will not be channeled properly. As a result, further
strains and problems for the suburbs can be expected. In addition to the density of development in suburbia increasing with
the expanding population, suburbia will also grow outward.
The result will be that the open country and rural communities
that now lie beyond our present suburbs will soon be overcome by suburban sprawl. This will cause suburbia to become
even more awkward and unwieldy.

"If present trends continue, those millions of new houses will inundate the countryside with sprawling, chaotic settlements on a scale dwarfing anything seen up to now," writes Edmund K. Faltermayer. He does not predict that soon there will be no more land to stand on. "The danger," he says, "is rather that the country's metropolitan complexes will become so spread out as to destroy their liveability."[13]

The urbanized area surrounding the twin cities of Minneapolis and St. Paul, at the current rate of expansion, will spread over more than a thousand square miles by the year 2000, more than three times the area it presently occupies. The suburbs are rapidly coming to be regarded as combining the worst, not the best, of city and country.

Until very recently it was possible to talk of a city and a suburb. But the United States is changing, and the growing urban and suburban landscapes are overlapping each other. A few years ago a French geographer named Jean Gottmann headed a field study of urbanization in America. Gottmann studied the eastern seaboard from Boston to Virginia. He stated in his report that the area he studied was a near-continuous strip of urban development. He called it a megalopolis and said it was the pattern of the future for many parts of the United States and eventually the rest of the world.[14]

Many people have misunderstood the term megalopolis to mean one huge super-city that is thickly populated and highly industrialized. It is instead a sort of patchwork of urban development, thick in some areas and thin in others. It is in essence a conglomeration of city and suburb. Megalopolis encloses several large cities and hundreds of small towns, villages, and communities. Each new community on the outskirts of an existing urban center helps to fill in the green areas. This process lengthens the distance to the country and increases the confusion and the problems of the developed areas. In the heavily developed areas a completely new kind of community, neither city nor country, is coming into being. According to architects and planners, the megalopolis is diffused, unplanned, and a chaotic, wasteful way to use land.[15]

One example of a suburban community that changed for the worse due to intensive, additional development is Forest Hills, New York. The district consists of two sectors; the Forest Hills Gardens area and Forest Hills proper. Each area contrasts with the other; the Gardens was developed by a planning board while the district proper was left to sprawl development. While Forest Hills Gardens has retained a residential character with a well-organized pattern of streets and homes, the district proper has been almost completely consumed by large, high-rise apartment dwellings that give the area a canyon-like appearance. [16] Today, parking is difficult to secure, schools are very overcrowded, parks are few in number, and traffic congestion is a serious problem. Largely responsible for this is the rapid increase in population that brought the total of 44,000 in 1941 to 125,000 people in 1963.

Similar to suburbanites elsewhere, the residents of Forest Hills fought additional development in their community when they saw it coming. But it turned out that they had only limited control over the destiny of the area. When they objected to the construction of an industrial park in the area, for example, they were successful, but their success only led the speculators to sell out their claim for an apartment complex. [17] This is typical of the non-planning and crisis management of suburban land.

The erratic, sprawl pattern of suburban development, which has occurred in the past and which likely will accelerate in the future, leaves large tracts of land open for speculation. It is the hope of most suburbanites that these lands will either be kept open or utilized for parks or recreational facilities. Politicians, meanwhile, seek a type of development that will yield an income for the local government so that the inevitable tax hike at the end of the year can be kept to a minimum. The speculators who own the land are merely interested in the most profitable type of development and they endeavor to use their money and influence to achieve this end. This is a free-for-all situation. When the land is finally developed, usually no one is satisfied.

Many suburbanites have come to recognize the problems involved in the sprawl dilemma and the futility of trying to solve these problems in the suburban atmosphere of separatism and confusion. This recognition on the part of suburbanites is an important component of suburbia in transition. It is reflected in an attitude survey that was conducted during the mid-1960's by the New York Regional Plan Association. In general terms, the results indicated that suburbanites desire improved public transportation, open space and esthetic controls, clustering of commercial and industrial areas near main arteries, integrated housing, and a transfer of some powers to a metropolitan-area agency in order to achieve these objectives. Specifically, 90 percent favored an all-encompassing regional transportation agency. In addition, more complete state control was sanctioned over public transportation as well as a degree of federal assistance.[18]

The suburban problems resulting from sprawl were initially tolerable to suburbanites. But they are losing their novelty and are rapidly reaching the point of unbearability. In addition to increased sensitivity to the immediate hardships caused by sprawl, some of the longer-term consequences of scattered, unplanned development are now being felt. As a result of far-flung development, roads, sewers, and telephone lines must all spread out accordingly to accommodate all residents of suburban areas. Usually this is simply a matter of "after the fact" insertion of these facilities. But since this is often done many years later, a complete conversion is necessary, which costs the average family three to five times more than it would have cost if these facilities had been installed during the initial development of the land. A change over from cesspools to a sewage system is just one example of this costly problem.

As suburban development grows in area and intensity, other problems are coming to the surface. The crime rate in suburbia, for example, is climbing at a rate six times greater than in the central cities.[19] It is a fact of police science that as density of development increases, crime increases more than proportionately. As with other services in suburbia, police departments are scattered, independent, and uncoordinated. Individually their resources and manpower available to fight crime are very limited. They are scarcely able to rise to the challenge of the increase in crime. In some areas, burglars, narcotics sellers, and other criminal types have a field day.

At the same time that there is growing recognition of the many problems inherent in suburbia, also becoming apparent is the fact that suburbia is responsible for many of the problems of the cities. City officials are starting to realize this at the same time that they are confessing that the cities cannot solve these problems on their own. Many cities that had hoped the federal government would step in and provide the necessary resources have been greatly disappointed.

On November 3, 1966, the Model Cities Program was in-
acted, signifying a step toward federal government participation
in the planning and rehabilitation of the cities in the United
States. The plan at the outset called for the Federal Housing
Authority to insure loans of up to 50 million dollars for community building funds, insurance of loans to subdivision con-
tractors for parks and schools, and long-term loans to enable
local governments to set aside lands for future use. [20] Eligibility
was granted to those cities which formulated a plan that included all income levels and prohibited discriminatory policies. [21]
Also required of cities was a structure for citizen participation
in the program. This unique blend of federal support and
local involvement was seen as combining a national centralized
effort with de-centralization of tasks at the grass-roots level.
This program looked very promising, but it proved to have many
limitations. First of all, only 70 cities out of the hundreds
applying could get this type of aid, [22] though many others des-
perately required it. Secondly, the 50 million dollars allocated
for the program turned out to be merely a token amount
when pitted against the massive problems of all of the cities in
the program. Criticism of the Model Cities Program soon came
from such city officials as Atlanta's Mayor Ivan Allen who
stated: "It is only a fraction of what is going to be required." [23]

Disappointed with the limited federal assistance offered to
cities, city officials have begun to look elsewhere for problem-
solving resources. Many eyes have turned to suburbia. Discussions have centered on the fact that suburbanites have abandoned the cities, yet maintain ties through their jobs there and
through their use of city facilities and services. It is being recognized that these people are an expense to the city, while they
contribute nothing to it. Suburbia indeed aggravates the problems
of the city by drawing industry away and by excluding the city
poor.

Aware of these things, city officials are now hard at work
trying to find means to make suburbia pay for the hardships it
has caused the city. One device that is becoming increasingly
popular is the city income tax which requires all people working
in the city to pay a graduated tax on their income, regardless of
where they live. Since the better jobs in the city are held by
suburbanites, their share of the taxes is very high. New York

City has found this method to be very effective. Cities have also been pushing state governments to set up special agencies to help solve their problems, using as revenue for this, taxes collected throughout the state, particularly from the more affluent areas. New York State recently created a statewide Urban Development Corporation that is striving to deal with the city housing crisis though a massive construction program.

The segregation and discrimination fostered by suburbia due to its traditional exclusion of poor people and minority members seems to be changing. Suburbia is becoming more heterogeneous. This is due to the higher density development of land (including construction of multi-family housing) which is taking place in suburbia and perhaps more importantly due to the pressures that have been exerted on suburbia to admit nonwhite, nonaffluent people. The federal government and the state governments are trying to desegregate the suburbs through various means. The Federal Housing Administration was set up to receive complaints of unfair housing practices. If anyone is turned down in his quest for federally assisted housing because of race, creed, or national origin, he can register a complaint with that agency. If the complaint is justified and negotiations fail to solve the problem, the government can cancel all federal aid to the real estate agent or bank involved. This is a strong weapon since FHA and GI home loans account for about 50 percent of all suburban development.[24]

The busing of children from a city or suburban slum area to white suburban schools has been justified on the grounds that it is an attempt to raise the performance level of minority children and in turn raise their aspirations.[25] Busing plans are usually designed and administered on the state level.

The federal government, meanwhile, has taken three approaches in an attempt to desegregate the suburbs. First of all, grants of money are awarded to those communities which cooperate with integration plans, but the grants are denied to those which do not cooperate. Secondly, special federal aid programs have been designed to achieve desegregation. Thirdly, the federal government has sought to create and support regional metropolitan agencies with jurisdiction over both cities and suburbs.[26] Dennis Wrong points out that the increasing heterogeneity of the suburbs resulting from these and other measures is a sign that the suburbs are becoming more urbanized.[27]

The population explosion in this country and its probable impact on suburbia were previously discussed. Another national trend that deserves consideration is the move toward apartment living. There are several factors responsible for this trend. Urban renewal programs in both cities and suburbs have played an important part. There are suburban communities such as Huntington Station, New York, where an urban renewal program is replacing 15 acres of single-family homes with 565 apartment units. Another factor behind the apartment trend is the high cost of land and home construction. Since 1951 land costs have gone up 16 percent per year, an overall rise of 300 percent. The financing of residential construction has doubled since 1961. In addition, the average cost of a building site increased 138 percent in the ten years prior to 1962. [28] Real estate taxes also went up approximately 50 percent from 1963 to 1969.[29] Finally, from 1951 to the present the average mortgage interest rate steadily climbed upward. [30] Considering bank rates and land and building costs, buying a house has become an exceedingly expensive proposition.

In the early 1950's multi-family housing comprised a mere 10 percent of all new housing. By 1962 a significant rise had taken place which brought this figure up to 40 percent.[31] In that year over 400,000 apartment units were built.[32]

In 1969 the median price of a new house in the United States was $26,000. Together with this price, the high mortgage and interest rates create an unbearable economic strain upon many, particularly young couples and retired people. As was pointed out, these are the age groups which are increasing most rapidly and which are creating the greatest demand for multi-family housing. Evidence of the apartment construction trend in suburbia is to be found everywhere. In suburban Nassau County, New York, for example, apartment permits now outnumber housing permits. In many areas apartment development accounts for up to 65 percent of all new construction.[33]

The boom of the modern apartment has been advanced in large part by the convenient assets that tenant living provides. These include close proximity to services, public transportation, shopping facilities, and recreation, things that most suburbanites have had to sacrifice. Because of the expense of purchasing and maintaining a home in today's inflationary economy, the trend toward apartment living can be expected to accelerate. Increasing land costs and decreasing building space in suburbia will have the effect of strengthening this trend.

Many of the current conditions and the resulting trends in the suburbs have made suburbia an area in transition. It is now appropriate to consider whether suburbia can survive in view of the pressures and strains that the present situation is creating. The next chapter addresses itself to this question.

## NOTES

1. Hauser, "How the Population Explosion is Changing the U.S.," *U.S. News and World Report*, No. 57, (August 31, 1964), p. 61.
2. *Ibid.*
3. *Ibid.*, p. 58.
4. *Ibid.*
5. *Ibid.*, p. 7.
6. *Ibid.*, p. 60.
7. *Ibid.*
8. *Ibid.*, p. 60.
9. J.J. Spengler, "Over-Population: Threat to America's Future," *Parents Magazine*, No. 43, (April, 1968), p. 42.
10. *Ibid.*, p. 42.
11. *Ibid.*, p. 42.
12. Hauser, *op. cit.*, p. 61.
13. Edmund Faltermayer, "We Can Cope With The Coming Suburban Explosion," *Fortune*, Vol. 74, (September, 1966), p. 149.
14. W. Landewiesche, "Suburbs Are Changing," *Readers Digest*, (November, 1962), p. 151.
15. "Suburbia The Target Area," *Wilson Library Bulletin*, (October, 1966), p. 173.
16. M. Polner, "Need for Suburban Planning," *America*, No. 112, (February 6, 1965), p. 188. Forest Hills was one of the original suburbs of New York City. It was annexed by New York City along with Queens county at the turn of the century.
17. *Ibid.*
18. "Suburbanites Cast Their Votes For City Planning," *Architectural Forum*, (December, 1963), p. 23.
19. "What's Wrong (and Right) With Our Suburbs?" *op. cit.*, p. 7.
20. "Face Lifting," *Newsweek*, (February 10, 1964), p. 67.
21. "Housing Program Under Fire," *Business Week*, (February 17, 1964), p. 32.
22. "Urban Renaissance or Boondoggle?" *Business Week*, (October 29, 1966), p. 141.
23. *Ibid.*, p. 142.
24. Don Oberdorfer and Milton MacKaye, "Will Negroes Crack The Suburbs?" *Saturday Evening Post*, Vol. 235, (December 22, 1962), p. 72.
25. Leonard Blumberg and Michael Lalli, "Little Ghettos: A Study of Negroes in the Suburbs," *Phylon*, Vol. 21, (Summer, 1966), p. 125.
26. "Governments Plan to Desegregate the Suburbs," *U.S. News and World Report*, Vol. 61, (October, 1966), p. 78.
27. Dennis Wrong, "Suburbs and the Myths of Suburbia," *Readings in Introductory Sociology*, (1967), pp. 358-364.
28. "Is Flight From Suburbs Starting?" *U.S. News and World Report*, Vol. 52, (June 11, 1962), p. 86.

29. "The Rush to Apartments," *U.S. News and World Report*, (December 8, 1969), p. 46.
30. *Ibid.*
31. *Ibid.*
32. "Is Flight From Suburbs Starting?" *op. cit.*, p. 86.
33. "The Rush to Apartments," *op. cit.*, p. 46.

# 9

# CAN SUBURBS SURVIVE?

No, suburbs cannot survive. At least not in the form in which they have existed.

Suburbia has been shown to be an artificial community, a community that separates work from living, the young from the old, whites from blacks, and rich from poor. An unnatural human settlement such as this with the many problems inherent in it cannot survive. And there is nothing special or sacred about suburbia that will make it an exception.

There are presently many social, economic, and political forces in the United States and its metropolitan areas that are clearly bent on suburbia's destruction. These forces have developed slowly over the years. Many now exist in advanced stages and their impact on suburbia is unmistakeable.

The forces that are militating against the survival of the suburbs are varied. Some of these have arisen from within suburbia itself, while others have come from without. Three types of forces are apparent. The first is the board area of social

forces. Included under this heading are factors related to people
— how they think and act and what their individual and group
characteristics are. One important trend here is the changing
age profile of suburban populations. Large segments of suburban
populations are coming to be comprised of the very young and
the old. This will affect the future of suburbs because these
particular age groups need, and will demand, city-type facilities
and conveniences that are not now present in the suburbs.
Sought by these growing suburban groups are such city-type
commodities as apartment houses, cultural and entertainment
facilities, and a good public transit system. These things cannot
simply be added to suburbia. Some fundamental and far-reaching
structural changes will have to precede them.

There are other social forces that also pose threatening consequences for suburbia. Two of these take the form of anti-
suburban sentiments which are gaining in national acceptance.
On the one hand there is a national reawakening of an old
American ideology, the concept of equalitarianism which places
citizens on a relatively equal standing with each other, ignoring
such individual differences as race, family background, and income level. The fact that this ideology, which was stated when
the country was founded and then was shelved for 200 years, is
again coming to the fore is reflected in recent public and private
actions. In the private realm a lessening of overt racial discrimination can be pointed to; in the public sphere the recent programs and policies attacking inequality stand as examples of this
revitalized ideology. Suburbia violates this ideology of equality
since its very image as a haven for the privileged is a blatant
contradiction to it.

The inequality that suburbia represents has given it many
enemies. Private groups and public agencies have said some very
uncomplimentary things about suburbia, and they have backed
up their words with actions. The NAACP recently launched a
nationwide campaign to open the suburbs to blacks and other
poor people. Their method is to appeal to the courts to elimin-
ate restrictive suburban zoning that denies to the city poor
the mobility to seek jobs in the suburbs because of limited
housing opportunities for them there.

Newly formed private groups are also taking up the cause.
Suburban Action Institute operating in the New York metropoli-

tan area is one such group. According to its directors, the Institute is "an ideological advocacy agency created to promote the use of suburban resources for solving metropolitan problems of race and poverty."[1] Several prominent urban planners and political activists have been attracted to work for this nonprofit organization which receives foundation grants for its support. Its directors are Paul Davidoff, a prominent professor of planning, and Neil Newton Gold, once a speech writer for former Senator Eugene McCarthy.

Suburban Action Institute has investigated several suburban communities that allegedly have their doors closed to the non-affluent. These investigations have been followed by lawsuits. One study completed by the Institute found that 68 percent of the land in Westchester County, located just outside of New York City, was zoned for building lots of at least one acre. This land, the study team found, accommodated only four percent of the county's nonwhite population, while 80 percent of the blacks lived on nine percent of the county's land. These findings received six columns of coverage in the Sunday *New York Times* when they were announced and became the basis of a subsequent lawsuit filed by the Institute.[2]

Government bodies are also getting into the act. Several states have passed laws or have established special agencies to deal with the unequal distribution of resources between cities and suburbs. A Massachusetts state law designed to force affluent suburbs to accept low- and middle-income housing recently went into effect amid the praise of urban supporters and predictions of disaster from suburban opponents. The law, nicknamed the "snob zoning bill," strips local communities of their traditional power to reject low- and middle-income developments on the ground that they conflict with established residential zoning. Instead, the communities will be required to set aside a specified portion of their land for such housing. Developers whose proposals are rejected by zoning boards will be able to appeal to a state appeals board that can override the local veto.[3]

In New York State, the Urban Development Corporation was recently established. One of the primary goals of this agency is to provide additional housing for the urban poor, both within and outside urban areas. An interview with the president of this State Corporation focused upon restrictive suburban policies and the problems created by these policies. He revealed the plans of his powerful agency to build middle-income and low-income housing on vacant suburban land even if it is necessary to override local zoning to accomplish this.[4]

Simultaneously, the federal government is bearing down on the suburbs. It is squarely facing the issue of whether the expenditure of billions of dollars of federal funds to rehabilitate the substandard housing of central cities and to encourage industry to locate within central cities — particularly within the slums — is justified in the face of the overwhelming trend toward decentralization of development and economic growth. A capsule history of federal policy toward the urban dilemma was recently written.

> In the early 1950's, recognition of the decline of the central city led to a concern with stemming it and with "bringing back" the fleeing middle class family to live in renewed and rehabilitated downtown neighborhoods. In the mid-1950's, the failures of the renewal program — its displacement of black and poor families, its failure to provide adequate relocation housing — brought a shift in policy toward rebuilding the ghettos for the benefit of their residents. This may be termed the "keep back" theory for ghetto residents. Now there is a growing recognition that both the "bring back" and the "keep back" theories are inadequate efforts to stem the tide of movement to the suburbs.[5]

The change in the position of the federal government is reflected in the findings of recently appointed federal commissions set up to study the urban crisis. The President's Committee on Urban Housing, the National Advisory Commission on Civil Disorders, and the National Commission on Urban Problems all pointed to the need for altering the suburbs for the benefit of the cities. Federal agencies have responded to this by encouraging the creation of metropolitan-area agencies to deal with urban problems and also by discouraging exclusionary suburban policies through threats to discontinue federally financed building plans and educational programs.

Among suburbanites, a change in their own attitudes about suburbia is taking place. There is a growing disenchantment with suburbia. It is a disillusionment which is being felt as the prophesized abundance of rewards and absence of problems of suburban life are not being experienced. The predicted rewards included fully adequate schools and public services, highly effective and responsive local government, and travel convenience far superior to that in the congested city.

But the prophesy of these rewards has not been fulfilled. At the same time, problems have been plaguing the suburbanite in abundance. These problems are more numerous and more city-like than were ever imagined. They include high taxes — taxes imposed on suburbanites not only by their own community but by the cities where they work, in the form of commuter taxes. Suburbia's high taxes reflect the inefficiency of public services there, an inefficiency caused by the spread of people and the proliferation of public facilities needed to serve them.

Other suburban problems exist in the form of both shortages and over-abundances. Shortages of parks, police, hospitals, and even water frequently exist. Many suburban areas are now wrestling with the present problem or future prospect of all of these deficiencies. Pessimistic predictions are being made, for example, about the ability of the water supply to meet the needs of rapidly growing suburban populations in many places. Even an area like suburban Long Island which is completely surrounded by water is faced with this problem. Southhampton, a relatively sparsely developed area on Long Island, recently released a planning study that said that the water supply of the area could support a population of only 90,000. The report pointed out that, if the present pattern of development continued, the population would someday pass 250,000.

Police protection presents another problem, a problem caused in suburbia by the difficulty of providing adequate police service to a highly scattered population. The insufficiency of recreation places in the suburbs is also cause for concern in many areas. This problem exists because speculators and builders have been gobbling up the choicest land in the best locations. By the time public officials realize what their constituents' park needs are, little land remains of the right type and in the proper location to satisfy these needs.

Yet at the same time that these shortages exist, there is an over-abundance of other things in suburbia, and this in turn is creating problems. In particular, there is an over-abundance of cars in suburbia. This produces congested roads and parking problems. Unfortunately, the great number of cars is a necessary suburban condition, necessary because of the absence of an adequate mass-transit system in the suburbs. This is not to say that some suburbs do not have good mass-transit systems. But those systems that are effective are usually good only for the suburbanite who travels to the city, not for the person who wants to get from one place to another within suburbia.

In addition to the large quantity of automobiles, suburbia is plagued by a multiplicity of local governments. Political scientist Robert Wood of M.I.T. in 1961 counted more than 1,400 of them in the New York metropolitan area alone.[6] There are more types of government in suburbia than most people realize. These include counties, cities, towns, villages, school districts, park districts, water districts, sewer districts, and all sorts of other "districts." If a public swimming pool is built, there will often be an administrative structure and a tax district created for it. Each of these units functions as a government normally does, and each functions independently. In the matter of taxing people and spending money, this independence has been a constant source of consternation to suburbanites.

The problems caused by the existence of such a vast number of small governments are many. To begin with, these units tend to duplicate some public services because of their overlapping jurisdictions, while each provides its services inefficiently because of its small-scale operation. Besides giving suburbanites services at higher costs than necessary, they give them unequal services. Some of the districts give better services than others, either because of more efficient operation or because of the chance existence of some large business or industry within their boundaries that gives them a broader tax base and better tax revenue.

There are apparently many problems coming to light that are making suburbanites dissatisfied with their communities. Other factors threatening the future of suburbia can be cited. In the realm of economic forces, there are indeed many trends that are impinging upon the survival of suburbs. One such trend is the decentralization of business and industry in metropolitan regions. Big business and industry are finding it lucrative to move from the cities to the suburbs. Here they find rich market areas and large labor pools. That this trend will change the shape of suburbs by making them more industrialized and business-oriented is apparent.

Another trend that looms ominously for suburbia is the advances being made in transportation technology. The immediate application of improved technology in this sphere will be to modernize outmoded suburban railroads, transforming them into the most rapid and efficient transit systems in metropolitan regions. What does this mean for suburbia? It means, for one thing, that parts of suburbia will be closer to the center of the city in travel-time than will be some outlying sections of the city. For example, after the modernization program of the Long Island Railroad is completed, it will take only 40 minutes to get from Manhattan to Huntington, a suburban community almost 50 miles outside of New York City. Meanwhile, it will continue to take an hour to travel on the New York City subways from places within the City, such as Jamaica, to Manhattan. This situation will spur intensive, urban type development in the portions of suburbia along the transportation network. These suburban areas may even become "downtown" sections for they will be attractive locales for high density residential and commercial development to meet the demands of people and businesses that depend on the city for their livelihood.

The final category of forces destined to transform suburbia are those political in nature. One important trend here is the redistribution of political power that is under way in this country. A greater share of the power is being obtained by minority groups, the poor, and the young. And it is the members of these groups who are among the greatest opponents of suburbia, for they are either excluded from suburbia or, when they are able to live there, their special needs go unrecognized. As the power of these people increases, they will be able to bring about change and reform in suburbia.

Another trend emerging as an anti-suburban political force is the expanding role of the federal and state governments in domestic affairs. The resources and responsibilities of the federal and state governments are certainly increasing, and this is happening at the expense of local governments. Local governments have traditionally been the protectors of the suburbs. As they become weaker, their ability to defend suburbia and prevent unwanted change there decreases. The federal and state governments, moreover, have been pressured to deal with the inequities of the suburbs. Influence has been exerted by way of grant awards and other devices in an effort to alter suburbia's social and physical complexion.

What has been presented is only a partial listing of anti-suburban forces now at work. There are many more. And all of these social, economic, and political forces will do their part in ending suburbia's era.

Amid all this speculation, however, one fact must not be overlooked. Suburbs are still growing, and people continue to come. The "suburban mystique" is apparently slow to die. But that too will pass. This mystique is fascination without factual foundation. For new suburbanites, the fascination is with the image of suburbia as a place devoid of city problems and devoted to the rewards of the good life. But the facts are telling a different story. They are exposing suburbia as a place with many city-type problems yet without the compensation of city comforts and conveniences.

The prediction of the passing of suburbia is in no way a lament for suburbia's demise. As has been shown, much criticism can and has been leveled at the suburban community. Suburbia has even been said to be immoral, and this claim has been supported with documentation. The word immoral is used in its broadest and most accurate sense. It refers to the fact that suburbia is damaging and unfair to human beings—to people who reside in it as well as to those who are excluded.

There is little question that by providing an isolated island for the white middle class fleeing from nonwhite cities, suburbia perpetuates segregation, causes inequality, and ultimately breeds race polarization and prejudice. Nor can it be denied that the spread of suburbanization causes governmental confusion, inefficiency, and ineffectiveness. The consequences of this municipal nightmare for suburbanites are inferior public services at higher service costs—costs that usually spiral over short periods of time.

With the problems of suburbia in mind, the question of whether suburbs *should* survive becomes intriguing. But this is beyond the scope of this analysis which has thus far concluded that suburbs *cannot* survive. Given our present concern, one final question is in order.

Who will be responsible for suburbia's final downfall? The

death-blow will not come from a single source. It will be the product of a conspiracy, one in which cities, states, the federal government, and even suburban factions will be a part. This powerful coalition will bring about measures that will insure the destruction of suburbia. The measures will include a drastic change in government zoning in the suburbs, a new priority for government projects that will focus on helping the non-affluent, and a restructuring of the metropolitan tax base to favor our faltering cities.

It should be made clear, finally, that suburbia will not pass away suddenly. It will expire over time, the process occurring gradually. And even after the end has come, the word "suburb" will still be used. People using it, however, will be referring to another type of area than that which now exists. It will be an area that resembles the city far more than the suburb as we now know it. It will be a place where the young and old, rich and poor, black and white will live; where there will be local jobs, after-work activities, and means for all to get to these; and where high-rise buildings, multi-type mass transit, industrial development, and "downtown" shopping areas will be commonplace. These will be the features of the communities surrounding cities after our present suburbs have disappeared. Without suburbia's artificial characteristics, the new communities will be much more natural than the suburb. And this will make their survival far more secure.

## NOTES

1. Paul and Linda Davidoff and Neil Newton Gold, "Suburban Action: Advocate Planning For an Open Society," *Journal of the American Institute of Planners*, Vol. 36, No. 1, (January, 1970), p. 14.
2. David K. Shipler, "Lawsuit to Challenge Suburban Zoning as Discriminatory Against the Poor," *The New York Times*, (June 29, 1969), p. 21.
3. "Massachusetts Will Open Suburbs to the Poor," *Newsday*, (November 18, 1969), p. 13.
4. Shipler, *op. cit.*
5. Davidoff and Gold, *op. cit.*, p. 15.
6. Robert C. Wood, *1400 Governments*, (Garden City, New York: Doubleday and Company, Inc. 1961).

# 10

# THE SUBURBS
# OF THE FUTURE

The suburbs, as we presently know them, will fade away. In their place will rise different communities that will take several forms.

Some of the present suburbs will simply become part of the cities which they border. In these areas the cost of land will rise to such an extent that tearing down relatively new structures to build high-rise buildings will be justified. As these areas resemble cities in appearance, problems, and needs, they will eventually be considered part of these cities and may even be annexed by the cities to form a larger and mutually more functional political entity.

Where annexation does not occur, several older suburbs will be forced into adopting many city features in an attempt to overcome their economic and transportation crises. The vehicle of urban redevelopment will be used to create "downtown" areas. These will be high-density areas similar to the downtown areas of cities. They will have many advantages of economy and efficiency, though they will all but destroy the low-density character of suburbia.

Similar to the emergence of suburban downtown areas, many concentrated "centers" will start to appear in the suburbs. These will be high intensity, multi-use areas developed on remaining vacant land in key locations of suburbia. They will be, in essence, small cities that will serve as focal points for varied suburban activities, including shopping, business, manufacturing, entertainment, higher education, and culture. A few of these centers will emerge by accident, but most will come about through conscious planning an conscientious government effort.

Twenty-three such centers were recently proposed for the New York metropolitan area by the New York Regional Plan Association, a private, nonprofit planning body supported by foundation funds. The centers were proposed "to combat urban sprawl, reverse segregated housing patterns, and conserve land." In proposing the centers, the Regional Plan Association predicted that they would eventually be demanded by suburbanites as the suburbs, under the pressure of expanding population growth, push so far to the perimeters of the region as to put them beyond reach of the city's job markets and cultural amenities.[1]

In addition to containing centers and downtown areas, the suburbs of the future will be forced to adopt the cluster principle in land development. The principle of cluster development is applied mostly to the construction of housing. It involves developing only part of a tract of land with houses on relatively small lots, and leaving a large portion undeveloped. This undeveloped section is preserved for open space and recreation. A typical application of cluster development would be building houses on one-quarter acre lots in a suburban area where half-acre lots are required. For each one-quarter acre lot developed, a lot the same size would be preserved as common open space. Ideally, all the development should be concentrated in a particular area rather than spread, so that the undeveloped land will form one contiguous greenway.

The cluster principle will be adopted by suburbia not only to meet the rising demand for open space and recreation areas, but also for economic reasons. Developers can offer homes at less cost when they build in the cluster manner because much of the land does not have to be bulldozed or covered with expensive concrete roads, curves, and sidewalks. While these homes can sell for less money, their resale value is excellent due to the enhanced quality of the environment. Suburban governments also benefit economically from cluster development since public services can be provided less expensively to homes in a cluster setting. Government further benefits because open land is preserved without the high cost of land acquisition. These benefits can be expected to stem the tide of rising taxes in the suburbs.

Cluster development, when used extensively, will result in a suburban community that will contain both city and country characteristics. The amount of land saved by the shorter distances between houses and the shorter roads will be "community" land. This open area is similar to the old "village green" or "village common" in New England towns. It belongs to everyone. This common ownership of land has in fact been one of the obstacles to cluster development, since people have to be convinced to give up a little land and privacy to gain a more functional community.[2]

One of the other features of future suburbs will be the adoption of comprehensive planning to guide development. Zoning and land development decisions in the future will not be made on the basis of emotional outcrys as to what is "good" or "bad" for the character of suburbia, but rather will be the product of thorough study and sound planning. The lack of planning in the past has led to many problems. The present population explosion, for example, is considered a crisis largely because of the lack of planning in land development policies. It has been argued that, were it not for this, the United States would have no population problem at all. In fact, even if the United States had the same high population density as England and Wales, the whole United States population could confortably be fitted into the State of Texas. Yet in England it is still possible, even with so large a population, to leave a city and drive in a short time to the country.

What was put into use in England and some other European countries has never been attempted in the United States. The Europeans have made national decisions on land use. They have planned ahead where housing would be built and, in fact, whether it was needed. In England, a "green belt" around London was legislated. Here is a stretch of ground that must be left as open land, serving several purposes; to protect farmlands close to city markets and to give city dwellers "breathing room" and recreation sities.

The need for strong planning in the United States has become recognized with the recent wave of concern over the preservation (and, in some instances, the restoration) of the purity and quality of the environment. Methods are now being sought to provide uniform standards for control of water supplies, sanitation, and other services on a regional basis. There is also a push for higher density zoning and conservation of land for parks in undeveloped areas.

Anthropologist Margaret Mead recently addressed a suburban audience and commented on the chaos and environmental threats posed by suburbia. She advised that environmental protection could be accomplished only if forceful and imaginative planning were done on a broad scale. The present course toward disaster in suburbia, she observed, was due to the fragmentation of planning and decision-making in suburbia and limited identification of suburbanites with the overall suburban community. She predicted that large-area planning in the future will be adopted of necessity and that land development decisions will be made on the basis of regional and long-term considerations.[3]

Long Island is one of the few suburban areas that has already embarked upon a vigorous region-wide planning program. From 1965 to 1970, dozens of economic, social, and environmental studies were undertaken by the Nassau-Suffolk Regional Planning Board.

Some of these studies were basic inventories, such as a thorough land-use survey, to measure existing conditions on Long Island. Other studies focused upon future projections of economic and population growth. Still others sought to test models of alternative development patterns. Out of this work emerged a comprehensive development plan which was published in the summer of 1970. [4] Let us review this plan, for it provides a glimpse into the future of the suburbs.

The plan begins with a discussion of the problems facing this suburban region. The key problems are listed as follows:

> Beaches and parks are overcrowded; fresh and marine waters are increasingly polluted; woodlands and fields are giving way to developments; older downtown areas are declining; and travel to New York City is frustrating, whether one uses the Long Island Railroad or the Long

Island Expressway. Although the vast majority of residents live in sound houses, housing problems exist for blacks, Puerto Ricans, and Indians; for welfare clients and migrant workers; for the young, the aged, and the large family of moderate income. [5]

From a discussion of problems, the report moves to a consideration of future projections of people, homes and jobs. Projections are also made of future needs for parks, transportation, housing, and jobs. It is projected that almost one-half million new homes will be needed in the next 15 years. Of these, about one-third should be apartment units, according to the plan. As the plan states, "The emphasis in the provision of new housing must shift away from single-family detached homes . . . ." The report also takes note of the transportation crisis and describes how suburbanites in the region have to contend with a transportation system that features bottlenecks on the highways, inefficient commuter railroad service, and infrequent and inaccessible buses. The heavy reliance upon the automobile is singled out as the chief cause of the transportation crisis. The following solution is proposed.

Two steps must be taken if this trend towards increasing use of the automobile is to be changed: first, the establishment of a highly efficient, frequent, and convenient mass transportation system consisting of coordinated rail and bus service; second, the grouping of all new land uses near transportation centers, at densities greater than those prevalent in the Island today.

The plan proceeds to set down a number of priorities based upon the analysis of problems and projections. Following this, the future development plan is presented in map and textual form. The plan emphasizes multi-family housing, wider housing choice, mass transportation, and higher development densities. A significant portion of new housing, according to the plan, should be built with public assistance. This is provided for in order "to assure decent homes for residents of low to middle income" and also because "the continued growth of industries and offices, which are among the Island's largest taxpayers, may depend on an adequate supply of housing for workers."

Three concepts form the overall developmental scheme provided by the plan — clusters, centers, and corridors. The principle of cluster development is recommended for application not only in the construction of housing subdivisions, but also in the creation of entire new neighborhoods. Since open space is identified as being sorely needed on Long Island, cluster development is seen as a way to save land from the bulldozer and the concrete mixer. Needed multi-family housing is also seen as being provided through the use of cluster development. The plan is relentless in its defense of multi-family housing. "Apartments relieve the mounting cost of public services, because the cost of public utilities, fire and police protection, and roads is lower per unit for apartments than for single family dwellings. In addition, new apartments on Long Island are a tax asset to schools as they generally pay more than three times as much in taxes as the cost of educating the children from these units."

The concept of centers is another key ingredient of the plan. Two types of centers are provided for: the single-use center and the multi-use center. An example of a single-use center is a transportation center. Several of these are planned at points where the main line of the commuter railroad passes major highway arteries. With ample parking facilities at these centers, the mass transit advocate would be able to abandon his automobile each day at these convenient locations.

A variety of land uses and activities would be contained in the multi-use centers. These would be the future downtown areas and the small cities in the suburbs. They would contain major concentrations of housing, stores, offices, industry, transportation, educational and recreational facilities, entertainment, and special services.

Also incorporated in the plan is the concept of corridors. This concept calls for major concentration of development, particularly nonresidential development, along a spine running down the center of Long Island. The idea is explained as follows:

> Consider the geography of Nassau and Suffolk Counties — long, narrow, attached at one end to one of the world's major cities, surrounded everywhere else by water. Clearly, the most valuable recreation land is at the waterfront; the best location for housing is adjacent to the recreation areas. Equally clearly, the most logical location for industry and other employment is along the center spine of the Island, close to its major transportation facilities. In this location, equi-distant from both the north and the

south shores, jobs will be most accessible to residents, yet the inevitable harmful effects of industry — noise, traffic, — will be minimized.

Although the corridor concept applies particularly well to Long Island because of the area's geography, it would also seem to apply to other suburban regions. For in most regions there is a central commuter line that emanates from a main city and runs like a spine through suburbia.

The Nassau-Suffolk plan offers insight into the future of the American suburb. For it is not a plan that detaches itself from reality and attempts to paint a utopian picture. Rather it is a study of existing trends, a projection of where these trends will lead, and a statement of what must be done to solve major suburban problems.

Aside from the form our present suburbs will take in the future, the development of those areas around the cities where nothing now exists must be considered. These areas will be planned and developed from scratch. Many of these areas will be developed as self-contained communities providing, right from the beginning, for industry, mass transit, downtowns, multi-family housing, recreation, and open space. These types of settlements have already been developed in certain regions, and are referred to as "new towns."

To help relieve population pressure on London and other British cities and to prevent urban sprawl, England began building "new towns" shortly after World War II. Only in the past decade has the idea of the "new town" been seriously considered as an alternative to the traditional suburb in this Country. Though it has thus far been attempted by only a few private builders with virtually no help from the government, this appears to be changing. The government has recently endorsed this concept and has provided funds to implement it on a large scale.[6]

One of the best examples of a "new town" in this Country is Columbia, Maryland, located midway between Baltimore and Washington. It is within commuting distance of both of these major cities. This "new town" opened its doors to residents in 1967. It is being built for a population of 125,000, which it is projected to contain by 1980.

Columbia is slightly larger than Manhattan Island. Of its

15,000 acres, 3,200 have been set aside for open space for use as parks, lakes, pathways and woodlands, school playing fields, and golf courses. Columbia will consist of seven villages grouped about a downtown section. Each village will have a population of 10,000 to 15,000 and each will be divided into several neighborhoods.[7]

A village center in Columbia contains stores, a supermarket, offices, a middle and high school, a community hall, and recreational and religious facilities. Housing is also provided in the village centers, such as in Harper's Choice Village Center where several studio-like, balcony apartments are being built over the stores.[8] Downtown Columbia will be the location of one of the largest enclosed shopping malls in the nation. Five department stores and 200 shops are planned for the retail heart of the city. There also will be restaurants, theaters, and offices in the downtown mall.

Columbia is considered one of the more successful "new towns" for it has grown rapidly and has managed to stick very close to its original objectives of being a self-contained community. A few "new towns" have run into some trouble. Reston, Virginia, for example, has yielded to the tight money market and has all but dispensed with its plan to include a proportionate share of low-income housing in its building program. Litchfield Park, located outside of Phoenix, Arizona, was begun in 1966 as a "new town" that would eventually house 100,000 people and would contain "all the things needed to sustain them." After four years of construction work, only 400 new units have been built in the first of twelve villages. Some 230 families had houses custom built. But for merchant builders, the timing was wrong. Tight money kept them away, creating severe inventory problems in Litchfield.[9]

Despite a few setbacks in the 1960's, the future of "new towns" as replacements for traditional suburbs seems bright. There are indications that the "new towns" that have developed according to their plans are working very well. And the federal government has recently taken measures to spur "new town" development. A legislative bill introduced in 1970 provides for long-term, deferred-payment loans for "new town" developers. Such long-term financing, with deferred payments, will lift the heavy debt-service burden from developers' shoulders until a "new town" begins to pay off. Also under the bill, the urban renewal program is extended to cover the development of undeveloped land. Finally, the bill permits the federal government to designate "accelerated growth centers" — smaller towns near larger cities that could be stimulated to grow and absorb much of the present suburban sprawl.[10]

The suburbs of the future will be essentially of two varieties. First there will be the existing suburban areas, changed beyond recognition through the clustering of high density development and the concentration of city-type facilities in satellite centers. The other variety will be the "new town." This will appear wherever there is a large mass of undeveloped land that has not yet been penetrated by urban sprawl, but that is close enough to a major city to become part of a metropolitan economy. These two types of communities will replace the traditional suburbs which will someday be looked upon as outmoded artifacts of life in the mid-twentieth century.

## NOTES

1. Richard Phalon, "Planners Urging 23 Urban Centers in New York Area," *New York Times*, (November 18, 1968), p. 1.
2. "Great Housing Rush of 1968," *Business Week*, (February 10, 1968), p. 22.
3. "Anthropologist Says Long Island Could Be Model," *Newsday*, (August 27, 1969), p. 17.
4. Nassau-Suffolk Regional Planning Board, Nassau-Suffolk Comprehensive Development Plan Summary, July, 1970.
5. *Ibid.*
6. "New Towns Rise on the Hill," *Business Week*, (February 7, 1970), p. 96.
7. *Welcome to Columbia: A Visitors Guide* (no date or publisher given), p. 1.
8. *Columbia Today*, (July, 1970), p. 4.
9. "Why New Towns Boom or Fall Flat," *Business Week*, (November 15, 1969), pp. 149-150.
10. "New Towns Rise on the Hill," *op. cit.*

# BIBLIOGRAPHY

Abrams, Charles. *Forbidden Neighbors*. New York: Harper and Brothers, 1951.

"All Around the Town." *Changing Times*. Vol. 16, (December, 1967), pp. 31-32.

Bacon, Edmund N. *American Homes and Neighborhoods, City & Country*. Annals of the American Academy of Political and Social Science, (July 1, 1968), pp. 117-129.

Beattie, W.M. Jr. "Plight of Older People in Urban Areas." *Aging*, (January, 1968), p. 10.

Berger, Bennett M. "Suburbia and the American Dream." *The Public Interest*. Vol. 2, (Winter, 1966), pp. 80-92.

Berger, Bennett N. "The Myth of Suburbia," *Journal of Social Issues*. Vol. 171, (1961), pp. 38-49.

Berger, Bennett. *Working Class Suburb*. Berkeley and Los Angeles: University of California Press, 1960.

Birkhead, Guthrie S. (ed.). *Metropolitan Issues: Social, Governmental, Fiscal*. Syracuse, New York: Maxwell Graduate School of Citizenship and Public Affairs, 1962.

Blake, P. "Speaking Out: The Suburbs are a Mess; Excerpt From God's Own Junkyard." *Saturday Evening Post*. Vol. 14, (October 5, 1963), p. 236.

Blumberg, Leonard and Lalli, Michael. "Little Ghettos: A Study of Negroes in the Suburbs." *Phylon*. Vol. 21, (Summer, 1966), pp. 117-131.

139

Bogue, David Joseph. *Metropolitan Decentralization: A Study of Differential Growth.* New York: Oxford University Press, 1950.

Bollens, John. *The Metropolis: Its People, Politics and Economic Life.* New York: Harper and Row, 1965.

Bottomore, T.B. *Elites and Society.* New York: Basic Books, Inc., 1964, pp. 28-33.

Breslin, J. "Speaking Out: I Hate the Suburbs." *Saturday Evening Post.* Vol. 10, (September 24, 1966), p. 239.

Brown, Lan. "Cumbermuld — A New Urbanity." *New Society.* Vol. 93, (July 9, 1964), pp. 11-12.

Burtt, E.J. Jr. "Workers Adapt to Plant Relocation in Suburbia." *Monthly Labor Review.* Vol. 91, (April, 1968), pp. 1-5.

Carver, Humphrey. *Cities in The Suburbs.* Toronto, Ontario: University of Toronto Press, 1962.

Chamberlin, A. "When the Russians Try to Invade Suburbia." *Saturday Evening Post.* Vol. 236, (August 24, 1963), pp. 28-9.

"Changing Suburbs." *Architectural Forum.* Vol. 114, (January, 1961), pp. 47-104.

Chinitz, Benjamin. *City and Suburb: The Economics of Metropolitan Growth.* Englewood Cliffs, New Jersey: Prentice-Hall, 1965.

"Cities Crowding: Countryside Losing." *U.S. News and World Report.* (May 7, 1962), pp. 76-80.

"City: Starting From Scratch." *Time.* Vol. 93, (March 7, 1969), pp. 25-26.

Clark, Samuel Delbert. *The Suburban Society.* Toronto: University of Toronto Press, 1966.

Conant, James Bryant. *Slums and Suburbs.* New York: McGraw-Hill, 1961.

Coulter, Phillip B. (ed.). *Politics of Metropolitan Areas.* New York: Thomas Y. Crowell Company, 1967.

Cox, Flip and Bricksur, Leo. *Retail Decentralization.* 1967.

Crouch, Winston W. "Conflict and Co-operation Among Local Governments in the Metropolis." Annals of the American Academy of Political and Social Science, Vol. 359, (May, 1965), pp. 60-70.

Deutscher, Irwin and Thompson, Elizabeth. *Down Among the People: Encounters with the Poor.* New York: Basic Books, Inc., 1968, pp. 127-54.

Dickinson, William B. "Suburban Migration." *Educational Research Report.* (July 20, 1960), pp. 525-541.

Dobriner, William Mann. *Class In Suburbia.* Englewood Cliffs, New Jersey: Prentice-Hall, 1963.

Dobriner, William Mann. (ed.). *The Suburban Community.* New York: Putnam, 1958.

Donaldson, Scott. *The Suburban Myth.* New York: Columbia University Press, 1969.

Douglass, Louis. "Elements of Shopping Center Design: Check List and Commentary." *Architectural Record.* Vol. 139, (April, 1966), pp. 160-163.

Duhl, Leonard. *The Urban Condition.* New York: Basic Books, Inc., 1963.

Duncan, Otis and Reiss, Albert Jr., *Social Characteristics of Urban and Rural Communities.* New York: John Wiley and Sons, Inc., 1956, Chp. 12, 14.

Duvall, E.M. and Blakely, R.J. "Lonely Youth of Suburbia." *PTA Magazine.* Vol. 55, (April, 1961), pp. 14-16.

Dye, Thomas R. "City-Suburban Social Distance and Public Policy." *Social Forces.* Vol. 44, No. 1, (September, 1965), pp. 100-106.

Dye, Thomas R. "Popular Images of Decision-Making in Suburban Communities." *Sociology and Social Research.* Vol. 47, No. 1, (October, 1962), pp. 75-83.

Eppley, G.G. "Fringe Area Problems." *Recreation*. Vol. 52, (November, 1969), p. 369.

Faltermayer, E.K. "We Can Cope With the Coming Suburban Explosion." *Fortune*. Vol. 74, (September, 1966), pp. 147-151.

Farley, Reynolds. "Suburban Persistence." *American Sociological Review*. Vol. 29, No. 1, (February, 1964), pp. 38-47.

"Feud Between City and Suburb." *Life*. Vol. 61, (July 1, 1966).

Fisher, Alena W. and Fairbank, Robert P. "The Politics of Property Taxation." *Administrative Science Quarterly*. Vol. 1, (June, 1967), pp. 48-71.

Fort, Bob. "City and Country Consider Consolidation." *American City*. Vol. 83, (August, 1968), pp. 48-49.

Francis, Roy G. "Family Strategy in Middle Class Suburbia." *Sociology Inquiry*. Vol. 33, (Spring, 1963), pp. 157-164.

Gans, Herbert J. "An Anatomy of Suburbia." *New Society*. Vol. 10, No. 261, (September 28, 1967), pp. 423-431.

Gans, Herbert J. "Planning and Social Life: Friendship and Neighbor Relations in Suburban Communities." *Journal of the American Institute of Planners*. Vol. 27, (May, 1961), pp. 134-140.

Gans, Herbert J. *The Levittowners*. New York: Pantheon, 1967.

Gans, Herbert J. "White Exodus to Suburbia Steps Up." *New York Times Magazine*. (January 7, 1968), pp. 24-25.

"Genial Suburb." *Esquire*. Vol. 64, (December, 1965), pp. 220-221.

Goldstein, Sidney. "Urban and Rural Differentials in Consumer Patterns of the Aged." *Rural Sociology*. Vol. 31, No. 3, (September, 1966), pp. 333-346.

Goldstein, Sidney and Mayer, Kurt B. "The Impact of Migration on the Socio-Economic Structure of Cities and Suburbs." *Sociology and Social Research*. Vol. 50, No. 1, (October, 1965), pp. 5-23.

Gorden, Albert·A. "Jews in Suburbia." Boston: *Beacon*. (1959).

Gordon, Harrison. "Law and Living Room." *Saturday Review*. Vol. 51, (August 3, 1968), pp. 48-49.

Gordon, R. "Split Level Trap." *Good Housekeeping*. Vol. 152, (January, 1961), pp. 35-50.

"Government's Plan to Desegregate the Suburbs." *U.S. News and World Report*. Vol. 61, (October, 1966), pp. 76-78.

Grant, Daniel R. "The Metropolitan Government Approach: Should, Can and Will It Prevail?" *Urban Affairs Quarterly*. Vol. 33, (March, 1968), pp. 103-110.

Greer, Scott. *Metropolities, A Study of Political Culture*. New York: John Wiley and Sons, Inc., 1963.

Hallenbeck, W.C. *American Urban Communities*. New York: Harper and Brothers Publishers, 1951, p. 202.

Herzog, A. "Shops, Culture, Centers, and More." *New York Times Magazine*. (November 18, 1962), pp. 34-35.

Heusinkvelo, Helow and Musson, N. *Best Places to Live When You Retire*. 1968.

Hill, M.E. "Reflection on Rejection." *America*. Vol. 103, (July 30, 1960), pp. 497-498.

Hoover, Edgar and Vernon, Raymond. *Anatomy of a Metropolis*. Garden City, New York: Doubleday and Co., 1959.

"How to Bring Suburbia Joys to Town." *House and Garden*. Vol. 125, (May, 1964), pp. 168-169.

"How to Woo, and Win Industry: A Symposium." *Nation's Business*. Vol. 56, (November, 1968), pp. 82-86.

Hurley, N.P. "Case For Suburbia." *Commonweal*. Vol. 70, (August 28, 1959), pp. 439-41.

"Is Flight From Suburbs Starting?" *U.S. News and World Report*. Vol. 52, (June 11, 1962), pp. 86-89.

Kahl, Joseph. *The American Class Structure*. New York: Rinehart and Co., 1957, pp. 428-502.

Keats, J. "Anyone for Elegance." *Coronet*. Vol. 45, (March, 1959), pp. 156-63.

Keats, J. "Compulsive Suburbia." *The Atantic*. Vol. 205, (April, 1960), pp. 47-50.

Klaman, Saul B. "Public/Private Approaches to Urban Mortgage and Housing Problems." *Law and Contemporary Problems*. Vol. 32, No. 1, (Spring, 1967), pp. 250-265.

Lansing, John B. and Hendricks, Gary. *Automobile Ownership and Residential Density*. University of Michigan, Institute for Social Research, 1967.

Lazerwitz, Bernard. "Metropolitan Community Residential Belts 1950-1956." *American Sociological Review*. Vol. 25, No. 2, (April, 1960), pp. 245-252.

Legett, John. *Class, Race and Labor*. New York: Oxford University Press, 1968, pp. 96-118.

Lieberson, Stanley, "Suburbs and Ethnic Residential Patterns." *American Journal of Sociology*. Vol. 67, No. 6, (May, 1962), pp. 673-681.

Lindholm, Richard W. (ed.). *Property Taxation — USA*. University of Wisconsin, 1967.

Lloyd, G.D. "Cluster Zoning: One Step Toward a Better Suburbia." *American Homes*. Vol. 67, (June, 1964), pp. 46-47.

Loeuerstein, Louis K. *Taxation of Residence and Work Places in Urban Areas*. Scarecrow, 1965.

Lowe, Jeanne R. "Race, Jobs and Cities: What Business Can Do." *Saturday Review*. Vol. 52, (January 11, 1969), pp. 27-30.

Lundberg, Ferdinand. *The Rich and The Super-Rich*. New York: Lyle Stuart Inc., 1968.

Makielski, S. Jr., *Politics of Zoning: New York, 1916-1960*. New York: Columbia University Press, 1965.

Manis, J.G. and Stine, L.C. "Suburban Residence and Political Behavior." *Public Opinion Quarterly*. Vol. 22, No. 4, (Winter, 1958-59), pp. 483-489.

Marris, Peter. *Dilemmas of Social Reform*. New York: Atherton Press, 1962, pp. 894-940.

"Mass Transit, Today and Tomorrow." *American City*. Vol. 83, No. 6, (March, 1968).

McBroom, Paul. "New Towns: An Urban Frontier." *Science News*. Vol. 92, (July 15, 1967), pp. 64-65.

McKain, Walter, Jr. "Rural Suburbs and Their People." *Journal of Co-operative Extension*. Vol. 1, No. 2, (Summer, 1963), pp. 76-84.

McKee, Raymond. *Suburbs*. Boston: Houghton Mifflin, 1957, pp. 132-133.

Mead, M. "View From the Picture Window — Are The Suburbs Really Perfect?" *Redbook*. Vol. 38, (October, 1967), p. 129.

Moskin, J.R. "Suburbs: Made to Order For Crime." *Look*. Vol. 30, (May 31, 1966), pp. 20-27.

Mumford, Lewis. *The City in History*. New York: Harcourt, Brace, and World, 1961.

"Negro Cities, White Suburbs: It's The Prospect For The Year 2000." *U.S. News and World Report*. Vol. 60, (February 21, 1966), pp. 72-73.

"New Towns: Answer to Urban Sprawl?" *U.S. News and World Report*. Vol. 60, (February 14, 1966), pp. 114-16.

Newman, D.K. "Decentralization of Jobs." *Monthly Labor Review*. Vol. 90, (May, 1967), pp. 7-13.

Oberdorfer D. and MacKaye, M. "Will Negroes Crack the Suburbs?" *Saturday Evening Post*. Vol. 235, (December 22, 1962), pp. 71-73.

Osborn, Frederic V. and Whittick, Arnold. *The New Town: The Answer to Megalopolis*. New York: McGraw-Hill, 1963.

Ostorbind, Carter C. (ed.). *Aging: A Regional Appraisal*. University of Florida, 1961.

Otten, Alan L. "The Voice of Suburbia — One-Man, One-Vote Edict Helps Environs More than Cities." *Wall Street Journal*. Vol. 167, (January 31, 1966), p. 12.

Pierce, P. "Crime in the Suburbs." *Ebony*. Vol. 20, (August, 1965), pp. 167-72.

Purdom, Charles B. *Building of Satellite Towns*. Hillary, 1949.

"Quit Picking on Suburbia." *Changing Times*. Vol. 17, (October, 1963), pp. 34-36.

Raby, William. *Income Tax and Business Decisions*. Englewood Cliffs, New Jersey: Prentice-Hall, 1964.

Rapkin, Chostor and Grigsby, W.G. *Demand For Housing in Racially-Mixed Areas*. University of California, 1960.

Rekjuss, John A. "Metropolitan Government: Four Views." *Urban Affairs Quarterly*. (June, 1968), pp. 91-112.

Riesmann, David. "Flight and Search in the New Suburbs." *International Rural Community Development*. Vol. 4, (1959), pp. 123-136.

"Rise of Suburban Power." *Christian Century*. Vol. 84, (October 11, 1967), pp. 1275-1276.

"Rise of the New Cities." *Nation's Business*. Vol. 56, (August, 1968), pp. 72-76.

Rohrer, Wayne C. and Hirzel, Robert. "A Methodological Note on Demographic Analyses of the Rural-Urban Fringe." *Rural Sociology*. Vol. 22, No. 1, (1957), pp. 71-73.

"Roots of Home." *Time*. Vol. 75, (June 20, 1960), pp. 14-18.

Sanford, Nevitt. *The American College*. New York: John Wiley and Sons, Inc., 1962, pp. 894-940.

Schnore, Leo F. "Socio-Economic Status of Cities and Suburbs." *American Sociology Review*. Vol. 28, No. 1, (February, 1963), pp. 76-85.

Schnore, Leo F. "The Social and Economic Characteristics of American Suburbs." *Sociology Quarterly*. Vol. 4, No. 2, (Spring, 1963), pp. 122-134.

Schnore, Leo F. *The Urban Scene*. New York: The Free Press, 1965.

Schol, Sr. "Confusion in the Suburbs." Vol. 77, (October 26, 1960), pp. 12-14.

"Segregation the Law Doesn't Stop — In The Rush To The Suburbs, Negroes Are Staying Behind." *U.S. News and World Report*. Vol. 50, (April 10, 1961), pp. 60-61.

Senn, Milton. "Race, Religion & Suburbia." *Journal of Intergroup Relation*. Vol. 3, No. 2, (1962), pp. 159-170.

Soter, Edward. *Miami Metropolitan Experiment: A Metropolitan Active Study*. Garden City, New York: Doubleday and Co., 1966, (rev. ed.)

Spectorsky, Auguste C. *The Exurbanites*. Philadelphia: Lippincott, 1955.

Stauber, Richard L. "The Science of Suburbia: A Case For the Sociology of Knowledge." *Kansas Journal of Sociology*. Vol. 1, No. 3, (1965), pp. 137-154.

Stein, Clarence S. *Toward New Towns for America*. New York: Reinhold, 1957.

Stein, Maurice. *The Eclipse of Community*. Princeton, New Jersey: Princeton University Press, 1960.

Strauss, Anselm. *The American City*. Chicago: Aldine Publishers Company, 1968.

Strauss, Anselm. "The Changing Imagery of American City and Suburb." *Sociology Quarterly*. Vol. 1, No. 1, (January, 1960), pp. 15-24.

"Suburbia A Myth." *Science Digest.* Vol. 46, (December, 1959), p. 21.
"Suburbia: Lost Paradise." *America.* Vol. 107, (May 5, 1962), p. 199.
"Suburbs Cut Cities Down to Size." *Business Week.* (June 18, 1960), p. 64.
"The Changing Suburbs." *Architectural Forum.* Vol. 114, (January, 1961), pp. 47-104.
"Tomorrow's Suburbs: Better Living For Less Money." *Changing Times.* Vol. 18, (April, 1964), pp. 23-24.
"Typical White Suburbanite." *Ebony.* Vol. 20, (August, 1965), pp. 123-126.
"Upgrading Downtown: Downtown Renewal." *Architectural Record.* Vol. 137, (June, 1965), pp. 175-190.
Veatre, Francis T. "Local Initiatives in Urban Industrial Development." *Urban Affairs Quarterly.* Vol. 2, No. 2, (December, 1966), pp. 53-68.
Vernon, Raymond. *Metropolis: 1985.* Garden City, New York: Doubleday and Co., 1963.
Vidich, Arthur J. and Bensman, Joseph. *Small Town in Mass Society.* Princeton, New Jersey: Princeton University Press, 1958.
Warner, Lloyd W. *et. al. The Social Life of a Modern Community.* New Haven: Yale University Press, 1946, pp. 97-129.
Warner, Lloyd and Meeker, Kenneth. *Social Class in America.* Chicago: Science Research Associates, 1949, pp. 34-8.
"Why They Chose The Suburb They Did." *American Home.* (April, 1962), pp. 35-39.
Wilson, James, (ed.). *The Metropolitan Enigma.* Cambridge, Massachusetts: Harvard University Press, 1968.
Winsborough, Hall. "An Ecological Approach To The Theory of Suburbanization." *American Journal of Sociology.* Vol. 68, No. 5, (March, 1963), pp. 565-570.
Winter, Gibson. *The Suburban Captivity of the Churches.* New York: Macmillan, 1962.
Wolf, J.R. "Stamford's Attempt to Integrate Suburbia." *Reporter.* Vol. 35, (December 29, 1966), p. 20.
Wood, Robert C. *1400 Governments.* Garden City, New York: Doubleday and Company, Inc., 1961.
Wood, Robert C. "Impotent Suburban Vote." *Nation.* Vol. 190, (March 26, 1960), pp. 271-274.
Wood, Robert C. "Suburbia." *Nation.* Vol. 188, (March 21, 1959), pp. 256-257.
Wood, Robert C. *Suburbia: Its People and Their Politics.* Boston: Houghton Mifflin, 1958.
"Wooing the Plants: Competitive Struggle Among States and Cities." *Time.* Vol. 88, (November 25, 1966), p. 110.
"Wooing White Collars to Suburbia: Office Parks." *Business Week.* (July 8, 1967), pp. 96-98.
Worster, C.B. "Can Cities Compete With Suburbia For Family Living." *Architectural Record.* Vol. 136, (December, 1964), pp. 149-156.
Wyden, Peter. "Suburbia's Coddled Kids." *Saturday Evening Post.* Vol. 233, (October 8, 1960), pp. 34-35.
Zikmund, Joseph. "Comparison of Political Attitude and Activity Pattern in Central Cities and Suburbs." *Public Opinion Quarterly.* Vol. 31, (Spring, 1967), pp. 69-75.

# INDEX

145